Seven from Heaven

The Miracle of the McCaughey Septuplets

Kenny and Bobbi McCaughey

With Gregg and Deborah Shaw Lewis

THOMAS NELSON PUBLISHERS
Nashville

Published in Nashville, Tennessee, by Thomas Nelson, Inc.

The Bible version used in this publication is THE NEW KING JAMES VERSION. Copyright © 1979, 1980, 1982, Thomas Nelson, Inc., Publishers.

"Children Are a Treasure from the Lord" by Jon Mohr, Phil Naish, and Greg Nelson. © Pamela Kay Music (ASCAP), Beckengus Music (ASCAP), BMG Songs (ASCAP), and Greg Nelson Music (BMI). Lyrics reprinted by permission of EMI Christian Music Publishing.

"Household of Faith" by John Rosasco and Brent Lamb. © 1983 Straightway Music (ASCAP). Lyrics reprinted by permission of EMI Christian Music Publishing.

Library of Congress Cataloging-in-Publication Data

McCaughey, Kenny.
    Seven from heaven : the miracle of the McCaughey septuplets / Kenny and Bobbi McCaughey with Gregg and Deborah Shaw Lewis.
        p.   cm.
    ISBN 0-7852-7049-3
    1. Septuplets—United States. 2. McCaughey, Kenny—Family. 3. McCaughey, Bobbi—Family. I. McCaughey, Bobbi. II. Lewis, Gregg A. III. Lewis, Deborah Shaw, 1951– . IV. Title.
    GN63.6.M33   1998
    618.25'0092—dc21
                                                    98-33949
                                                    CIP

Printed in the United States of America.

1 2 3 4 5 6 BVG 03 02 01 00 99 98

To our eight wonderful children,
who add to our joy each and every day
and
To our parents,
whose love and guidance have been an invaluable
source of strength

Kenny

I woke up in a foul mood. While a little rain in the night had seemed like a nice inauguration of our new camping equipment, a wet, drizzly morning didn't promise a very pleasant day.

I'd returned to our tent and was sitting on the air mattress wondering how long the rain was going to last when I spotted Bobbi through the door screen, walking across the campsite, holding her side as if she had indigestion. But when she knelt down to crawl back into the tent she just froze, doubled over as if she couldn't move.

"You okay, dearie?" I asked, suddenly realizing she was crying.

"No," she groaned.

When she didn't move or say anything else I crawled over toward her and asked, "What's wrong?"

"I'm not sure," she said, sobbing. "My side hurts."

I helped her ease onto her side on the sleeping bag. "Where does it hurt?"

"Here!" She guided my hand.

I could feel a hard knot in her abdomen. She moaned and inhaled sharply when I pushed on it.

"That's the side where your appendix would be," I told her. "You think it's appendicitis?"

"I don't know," she said. "It's also about where my ovary should be." We'd been told that one of the possible side effects of the fertility treatments we'd had could be overstimulated ovaries. In some cases enlarged ovaries had even been known to rupture.

"I think maybe we need to get you to the hospital," I told her. When she didn't protest or argue, I knew Bobbi must really be hurting.

If her appendix had ruptured, I realized we didn't have any

door of the tent, I wasn't certain I would be able to stand up again.

Outside in the misty, gray morning light, I saw that the fishermen had already left. Almost staggering with the pain, I headed across the little clearing toward the door of my sister's tent. "Barbara? Can I come in?"

"Sure," she replied. "What's up?"

"I've got a bad pain in my side. I want you to see what you can feel."

"Here, lie down." Barbara could tell I was hurting.

I got down on her sleeping bag.

"Where is it?" she asked.

"Right here." I pulled up my shirt and pointed. "Tell me what you feel."

When she prodded I winced violently.

"Sorry," she said.

"What do you think?"

"I don't know," she answered. "But there's definitely something in there. It feels hard. It hurts, huh?"

"Like nothing I've ever felt before!"

"That bad?"

"Yeah!"

"Have you told Kenny?"

"Not yet."

"Do you think you need to go to the hospital?"

"I don't know," I said. "Kenny's been looking forward to this camping trip all spring. I don't want to ruin the weekend for him. Maybe it'll just go away." But by that point I didn't really believe it would. With my sister's confirmation that there really was something there in my side, that I wasn't just imagining it, I got up and started back for my own tent.

Contents

Acknowledgments

*S*pecial thanks to Pastor Bob and Ginny Brown for your encouragement from the beginning. Your prayers and willingness to help have been boundless.

Thank you also to our incredible church family. Our lives would not be the same without you.

Much gratitude is due to all of our neighbors and friends who have given, and continue to give, so much time in dedication to our family.

We deeply appreciate each expression of kindness, each prayer, each act of generosity that has been shown to our family by so many people here in the United States and by those in many countries around the world.

Thank you also to many friends at the Ambassador Agency, who work so tirelessly on our behalf.

And to the excellent writing and publishing teams who have assisted us with this book, thank you!

Thank you most of all to our awesome God, without whom our existence would have no meaning. All we are and all we do is because of Him. Glory to His name.

One

A Weekend Gone Wrong

Kenny

For a long while only the chirping of crickets broke the silence surrounding me, then I slowly began to tune in to other subtler night sounds. Lying awake in the darkness, I listened to the steady breathing of my sleeping wife, five weeks pregnant, snuggled next to me in the cozy cocoon of our zipped-together sleeping bags. Beyond Bobbi, on the far side of the tent, I could just barely make out the soft stirrings of our sixteen-month-old daughter, Mikayla, as she shifted restlessly in her playpen. Outside a gentle breeze softly rustled the leaves high in the trees that lined the perimeter of our campsite.

I never have slept well on the first night of a camping trip. I'm a light sleeper under the best of circumstances. Outdoors, on the ground, separated from the elements only by thin nylon walls, it seemed as if every little noise was amplified. Yet, instead of letting my sleeplessness frustrate me, I found the sounds and sensations of camping to be a welcome change of pace from my regular routine. Being close to nature and that close to my family made me feel a little closer to God. Even lying awake in the dark, knowing I would be tired in the morning, there was still a sense that was more feeling than thought. A reassuring inner sensation that said, *All is right with the world tonight.*

Not even the first drops of rain splattering on the rain screen could dampen my spirits. I smiled to myself as I thought, *It never seems to fail. No matter what the forecast, it always rains on our camping trips. Why should this Memorial Day weekend be any different? I am not gonna let a little shower, or anything else, spoil our plans!*

Truth was, we were better equipped for wet-weather camping than ever before. Earlier in the spring my mother had given us a brand-new three-room cabin tent and then outfitted us with new sleeping bags and a nice, thick air mattress. Always before we'd shared a tent with Bobbi's sister and brother-in-law and made do with a pile of blankets and comforters to soften the hard ground. *So let it rain!* I thought. That would be a good first test of our new camping gear.

I was enjoying the soft sound of rainfall, appreciating my mom's generosity, and still trying to get to sleep when Bobbi roused enough to ask, "You awake?"

"Yeah."

"Is that rain?" she wanted to know.

"Just a little shower," I reassured her. "Go back to sleep."

When Bobbi rolled over to snuggle against me she groaned as if she was in pain.

"You all right?" I asked in a whisper.

"Mmm," was all I remember getting out of her. And it wasn't too much longer before the peaceful patter of gentle rainfall finally put me to sleep as well.

Bobbi

I'd fallen asleep much quicker than I usually did on the first night of a camping trip. Maybe I was more tired than I'd realized.

Between taking care of Mikayla and going through the normal daily routine, I'd spent most of my time and energy that Friday getting together everything we needed to take for a long weekend of camping. I had the car packed and ready to go at six that evening when Kenny got home from his job at Wright Chevrolet, the local car dealership in Carlisle, Iowa, where we live. Once Kenny changed clothes, all we had to do was strap Mikayla into her car seat and we were off.

As expected at the start of the summer's first holiday weekend, rush-hour getaway traffic was heavy in and around Des Moines. By the time we reached our destination, Jester State Park, about an hour northwest of the capital on the shore of Saylorville Lake, tents and trailers already packed all the designated campgrounds. Fortunately my sister Barbara and her husband, Neil, and my brother Pete and his wife, Linda, had been able to get away a little earlier in the afternoon. They were holding a spot for us in a primitive campsite almost a mile from the nearest running water. We would have to make do with outhouses, a picnic table, and a portable fire pit that was already ablaze when we pulled in. By the time we'd unloaded and added our tent to what became a semicircle of shelters around the fire, the sun had set. We cooked hot dogs over the fire for supper and then toasted marshmallows to make s'mores for dessert.

Once we got the children put to bed, we adults sat around the picnic table playing a friendly card game of Pit, enjoying one another's company and laughing a bit about the insanity of taking three pregnant women camping for a weekend in a place so far removed from flush toilets. My sister Barbara was five months pregnant with her third, and Pete and Linda were expecting their first child in less than a month. Kenny and I were still basking in the exciting news we'd gotten just a couple of weeks earlier; we were pregnant again!

We didn't play many hands of Pit before the fire died down and we chose to head for bed rather than add another log. Neil and Pete decided they would go fishing before breakfast. Kenny told them he hoped to sleep in and would go fishing with them later in the day. With those plans made, we all retired to our own tents.

I don't know when I fell asleep. But I remember being awakened sometime later with a sharp pain in my side. I mumbled something to Kenny who was still awake. Then I dozed off again before I roused to full consciousness.

I awakened the next time after dawn. My side still hurt. My first thought was, *I must have slept on it wrong.* But this was more than stiffness. *Maybe I strained or pulled a muscle loading the car yesterday or when we put up the tent in a hurry before dark last night.* But the pain was sharper and different from sore muscles.

I ran my hand along my side and pressed where I felt the discomfort. The sudden pain was excruciating. I quickly released the pressure and the pain decreased to a dull ache. I probed again with my fingers, more gingerly this time. I thought I could feel something hard or knotted when I pressed just below my ribs. That seemed to be the source of my pain.

Kenny had already dressed and taken a walk to the outhouse. But Mikayla was sound asleep; I didn't want to disturb her. So I slowly and silently slid out of the sleeping bag. As I stood, a wave of pain washed over me. When I stooped over to unzip the time to waste. If the problem was her ovary . . . I didn't even want to think about that possibility.

We immediately decided it would be easier to leave Mikayla with the aunts and uncles at the campground than to take her with us to a hospital emergency room. Figuring she'd be a lot happier if she got a full night's sleep, we didn't even wake her. We felt bad about not saying good-bye, but Barbara assured us, "Don't worry about Mikayla. She'll be fine. We'll take good care of her."

Wanting to get everything squared away there at camp, I told my sisters-in-law, "If it keeps raining, just take down our tent, fold it up, and put all our gear in one of your cars. I'll air it out later."

"We'll take care of everything," Barbara insisted. "You two just go."

We went.

I pushed our eight-year-old white Oldsmobile up to 75 miles per hour as we raced back toward Des Moines that dreary gray morning.

We didn't talk much. But I remember Bobbi saying a couple of times, "I don't want anything to happen to the baby."

And I remember praying little, silent sentence prayers as I drove. *Lord, be with Bobbi.*

Please Lord, don't let this be anything major.

Keep us safe, Lord.

Lord, help us get there in time.

Protect Bobbi and the baby, Lord.

Bobbi

The pain eased up somewhat on the drive to the hospital. I kept trying to think, *Maybe it really is nothing serious.* But in my heart I was still worried.

Kenny's first thought had been appendicitis. I hoped he was right. But the more I thought about it, the more I suspected the problem was with my ovary. That's why I kept thinking and I guess said out loud, "I don't want anything to happen to this baby!"

I remember thinking, *Lord, You've brought us this far. We're finally pregnant again. Please don't let anything happen to our baby!*

We decided to go straight to Iowa Lutheran Hospital, not because it was closest, but because we were familiar with it. That's where Mikayla had been born.

I didn't feel too bad when we pulled into a parking spot within a stone's throw from the emergency room door. But by the time we walked up to the admissions desk, I could hardly stand. The clerk took one look at me and called a nurse who brought a wheelchair and rolled me back to a tiny examination room while Kenny finished filling out the paperwork and giving our insurance information.

The nurse helped me onto the exam table and asked what I'd come in for. I told her about the pain. She asked if I was pregnant and when I told her I was, she took my pulse and blood pressure, recorded the results on a chart, and turned to leave. "The doctor will be right in," she informed me before she closed the door and disappeared.

Kenny finished with my admission and had been with me almost thirty minutes before a young doctor hurried in only to ask the same questions the nurse had asked and to recheck my vital signs. Then he ordered a blood test to determine my HCG levels (those are hormones indicative of pregnancy) and an abdominal ultrasound to check out the fetus and my internal organs. "When we get those results we'll have a lot better idea as to what the problem may be," he explained. And then he left without giving me any sort of physical exam.

In short order someone came in to draw blood. And then an aide wheeled me up to Radiology for the abdominal ultrasound. I didn't think the technician who did the ultrasound could find a baby. I'd had enough of these tests done during my pregnancy with Mikayla that I knew what to look for and I couldn't see anything on the screen. But I also knew that an abdominal ultrasound wasn't always conclusive this early in a pregnancy.

A half hour after I returned to the ER the doctor came in to tell me the official results of the tests. My HCG count did indeed indicate a pregnancy, but the ultrasound had not revealed any evidence in my uterus. "Your HCG levels are high enough that we should see something on the ultrasound. Since we can't, I'm concerned that your pain may be the result of an ectopic pregnancy. Who's your OB/GYN? We need to get them in here to take a look at you right away."

I gave him the name of the fertility specialist we'd been seeing. "Dr. Katherine Hauser."

"She doesn't have privileges here. But if you wanted to transfer over to Iowa Methodist she could treat you there."

Remembering the pain I'd experienced walking into Lutheran a couple of hours earlier, I thought, *I'm not going anywhere else.* "I really don't want to transfer."

"Have you ever gone to any other doctor on our staff?"

"Dr. Emge delivered our daughter, Mikayla," Kenny told him.

"Great," the ER doc responded. "We'll give Dr. Emge a call."

Our old OB must have been nearby because it wasn't very long before he walked into the ER exam room and greeted us both warmly. He glanced over my chart as we filled him in on what had happened. He felt my side and I winced in pain. "I know this isn't going to be comfortable," he told me apologetically, "but we're going to have to do an internal."

He called in a nurse who helped me lie back on the examining table. She held one of my hands and Kenny held the other. It's a wonder either of them had any circulation left by the time Dr. Emge concluded what was an excruciatingly painful exam.

"I'm not at all certain that what we have here is an ectopic pregnancy," Dr. Emge told us when he finished the exam. "I believe we need to do a laparoscopy to peek in there and be absolutely certain." He went on to explain what I already knew, that laparoscopic surgery was a fairly minor procedure involving some very small incisions through which the surgeons would insert a tiny visual probe that would give them a clear look at the problem. "I'm going to call Surgery and find out when the next OR is available," Dr. Emge said as he left the room.

By this time my parents, Bob and Peggy Hepworth, had arrived in the emergency room waiting area. They'd raced to the hospital after my brother Pete called home from Jester Park to tell them we'd gone to the hospital. "Why didn't you call us?" they asked Kenny when he'd gone out to talk to them. "We would have been glad to take Mikayla for you."

"Mikayla's fine," Kenny assured them. "And we didn't want to worry anyone before we found out what was wrong." He quickly relayed to them what had happened so far and then hurried back to the exam room to be with me.

We were still waiting to hear when the surgery would be when Kenny's dad and stepmother, Ken and Val McCaughey, arrived. After Kenny told them the doctor wanted to do an exploratory laparoscopy to rule out an ectopic pregnancy, Val asked if she could come back to the room with Kenny to see me.

To the two of us Val said, "Kenny told me it might be a tubal pregnancy. I just wanted you to know that if that's the case, Dad and I don't want you to worry. If you need more money for another round of Metrodin, we'll be glad to loan it to you."

Metrodin was an expensive fertility treatment—around $2,500 including all the tests and ultrasounds that went with it. Dad and Val had loaned us $1,000—the amount we thought our insurance wouldn't cover for the first round.

I thanked Val for the generous offer. I didn't tell her what I was thinking: *If something happens and this pregnancy doesn't work out, I don't think I want to go through the emotional roller coaster of fertility treatments again. I'm not sure I could!*

Val went back to the waiting room about the time Dr. Emge returned to tell us an operating room would be available in just a few minutes. After he left, a nurse came in to prep me for surgery. She did all the usual fun stuff: hooking me up to a catheter and helping me dress in one of those attractive hospital gowns. When an orderly came to wheel me to surgery, all our family who'd come to the hospital walked with us. They stood and prayed with Kenny and me as we waited outside the doors leading to the surgical wing of the hospital. We felt wonderfully supported. But also feeling a lot of pain, I was anxious to get started.

Several minutes passed before an OR nurse came out to apologize and tell us that Dr. Emge had been called into an emergency C-section. "I'm sorry," she informed us, "but you'll have to go back down to the ER to wait until he's done and can reschedule another operating room for your procedure."

It was back to Emergency to wait again. By this time it was well after noon and Kenny hadn't eaten all day. He and the others hurried off to the cafeteria for a quick bite.

They returned and we were still waiting when our minister,

Pastor Bob Brown, arrived. He prayed with us and stayed with the family until we got word that Dr. Emge and the OR were finally ready again.

Once again we all traipsed to the surgical unit where everyone wished me well as I was wheeled away through those big double doors. I recall lying on a table while the anesthesiologist hooked up an IV. And the last two things I remember before slipping into a peaceful, dreamless sleep were a nurse slipping leg warmers over my legs, and my prayer, *Lord, please keep the baby safe.*

Kenny

Watching Bobbi wheeled off to surgery was one of the worst moments of my life; waiting through that surgery was one of the hardest things I've ever done.

We'd expected the procedure to last maybe an hour, but that hour came and went. My mother and her husband, Kathy and Dave Addleman, arrived from Mason City to join the supportive family vigil. Still no word. I paced back and forth in the surgical waiting room the entire time, constantly sending up desperate little prayers: *Please, God, watch over Bobbi and protect our baby.*

Nearly two hours passed before Dr. Emge walked into the waiting area wearing his green scrubs. Above his lowered mask I was relieved to see a reassuring smile. "Everything went well," he said. "But the problem wasn't an ectopic pregnancy. Bobbi had an ovary that was so overstimulated it had swollen to the size of a softball. A cyst had developed on the ovary and had ruptured. We had to remove the ovary or she might have eventually bled to death.

"She's resting well. Her other ovary was also a little overstimulated but it seems to be fine. We didn't get close to the uterus, so the baby should be okay. When Bobbi's feeling better in a day or two, before she goes home, we'll do another, more effective ultrasound just to make sure. But I think mother and baby are both going to do just fine. You can go in to see her as soon as they get her situated in recovery."

That was wonderful news! I thanked the doctor profusely as I shook his hand.

Bobbi

When I woke up in recovery my first conscious thought was, *How can three little half-inch incisions hurt this much?* My second thought I voiced to the recovery room nurse who was checking my vital signs: "Is the baby okay?"

"You'll have to ask your doctor that question," the nurse told me. She disappeared about the time my parents and my eleven-year-old brother, Dennis, walked into the recovery room.

"How are you feeling?" they wanted to know.

I totally ignored their question to ask a more important one of my own. "Is the baby okay?"

"The doctor thinks the baby's going to be fine," Mom told me. I felt too tired for any real interaction. With the only question that mattered finally answered, I immediately drifted back to sleep. Dr. Emge came by to check on me a little later, but I was still so groggy he gave up and said, "We'll talk tomorrow."

I awakened Sunday morning feeling incredibly sore, yet surprisingly better. My spirits improved immensely when Kenny showed up after church carrying Mikayla in his arms. (Barbara and Neil had driven in from Jester Park Saturday evening to check on me and bring her home.) But I felt like crying when my daughter refused to hug me or have anything to do with me the entire time she was in the room.

I wanted to attribute her behavior to the fact that we were in a strange and unsettling place. But I couldn't help feeling that the shunning I received from my little girl was a sixteen-month-old's attempt to punish me for leaving her at Jester Park and not saying good-bye.

Kenny had Monday off as well. So instead of a long holiday weekend of camping in the great outdoors, Kenny spent much of the weekend camped beside my hospital bed. When I told him I was sorry about the way things had turned out, he laughed and told me we might have had a better weekend than Barbara and Neil and Pete and Linda. In the face of a severe storm warning Sunday afternoon they'd abandoned the campsite and come home for the night. "Neil and Pete drove back out to Jester Park today to take down their tents," he told me.

Dr. Emge came by to remove the dressing and check my incision, which was a lot more extensive than the tiny laparoscopy cuts I'd been expecting. "You're coming along so fine I expect you can plan to go home by tomorrow. But before you leave I want to do a vaginal ultrasound. Your HCG counts are definitely high enough now that we ought to be able to see something in there."

Tuesday morning a nurse brought in a pitcher of water and told me, "Drink as much of this as you can. When you feel like you've got to go to the bathroom, call me and we'll get someone to wheel you to Radiology for your ultrasound."

I knew from past experience that drinking lots of water can make for better definition in an abdominal ultrasound picture. But there had to be some kind of misunderstanding because Dr. Emge had said he was ordering a more accurate internal ultrasound. "I don't think I need to drink this," I tried to tell the nurse. "I'm not having that kind of procedure."

"All I know," she said, "is that Radiology wants you to drink as much water as you can hold."

It made no sense to me. But I wanted to get this last test over with—first, so I could know the baby was okay, and second, so I could get out of that hospital and go home to Kenny and Mikayla.

I dropped the argument and drank water until I was so full my incision hurt. Then I called the nurse and she had an orderly bring a wheelchair and take me to Radiology.

When he wheeled me into an ultrasound room and I spotted the technician my heart sank. I knew this guy. I remembered him from two years back when I had so many ultrasounds done before Mikayla was born. I never knew the man's name; he wasn't that personable. In fact he had always been so cold and impersonal that he refused to answer, and often merely ignored, my simplest questions. He seemed to resent any attempts I'd made at small talk.

Once I was lying on the table and he began to prepare for an abdominal ultrasound I said, "I think there's been some mistake. I just had major surgery Saturday. That's why Dr. Emge ordered a vaginal ultrasound, not an abdominal."

The tech clearly didn't like being questioned. "We always do an abdominal first," he replied tersely.

I decided to shut up and just get the test over with.

The technician got everything situated and turned on the machine. Then he spent a minute or two in silence carefully studying the screen of his monitor. I could see enough of the screen from where I was lying on the table to conclude that he wasn't spotting any baby.

"You can go to the bathroom now. We're going to have to do an internal in order to see anything," he said before he called the radiologist in. I wanted to scream, *That's what I've been trying to tell everyone.* But I bit my tongue and didn't say a word as they prepared for the second procedure.

When the screen lit up again both men hovered over the monitor studying it carefully. With two bodies in the way I could only see parts of the picture myself, but I noticed they were pointing to different areas on the screen.

They were just a few feet away, but the men whispered so softly I couldn't tell exactly what they were saying. I desperately wanted to ask, "What's wrong?" but they seemed so engrossed I kept quiet and tried to listen for the word *baby* or *fetus*. The longer this went on, the lower my spirits sank.

I finally thought I heard the word *cyst* about the time I realized they were counting. "Three . . . four . . . there's five."

Oh, no! Please, God, no! Not only are they not finding a baby, but they are seeing all these cysts. I'm never going to be able to have another baby!

Two

We Don't Want Seven Babies

Bobbi

I still didn't say anything. I just kept straining to hear what the technician and radiologist were saying. *They're counting again.* Then I heard one of them say the word *sac.*

That's when it dawned on me:

"You're counting babies, aren't you?" I asked.

"Yes," the technician replied.

"What number are you up to?"

"Five."

Five? Oh, my! That just can't be! The ultrasound Dr. Hauser did at the time I ovulated showed only three possible eggs.

I listened and watched them start at one side of the monitor and count their way across to the other side. Back and forth, they counted again and again.

"We think there are seven," they finally concluded. "We've counted seven sacs."

The radiologist hurried out of the room at that point and the technician began taking pictures of the ultrasound. I don't know why he took so many. I was on that table another twenty minutes while he clicked away.

Twenty eternity-lasting minutes to lie there and think: *What will Kenny say?* Then, *I don't want seven babies.* But most of all, *Get me out of here! I've got to talk to someone.*

Finally the technician spoke again, "I think we're finished. We'll have the radiologist look over these again. I'll call someone to take you back to your room."

I waited alone in the hallway for another ten minutes. Ten added minutes to worry and to wonder how I was going to tell Kenny. Ten more minutes of longing to be where I could talk to someone. Finally an orderly came to push my wheelchair to my room.

Once there, I grabbed the telephone and dialed my sister Barbara's phone number. No answer. I just *had* to tell someone. I called my mother at the Ben Franklin Store where she worked as a cashier. She answered the phone while waiting on customers in the checkout line.

"Hi, Mom," I greeted her.

"How did the ultrasound go?" she wanted to know. "Did they find the baby?"

"Ye-e-e-s," I answered.

Mom knew from the way I answered that something was up. "There's more than one?"

"Ye-e-e-s."

"How many?"

"Seven."

I heard a crashing sound on the other end of the line. My mother had dropped the phone. When it hit the floor, every cus-tomer in the front of the store who wasn't already watching her turned to see what was going on. Mom had to call another employee up to the front to take over her cash register, so she could go to the back room and sit down to talk to me. We talked for several more minutes, but I can't say I remember the rest of that conversation. We must have said something. But nothing else seemed to register. Everything seemed to focus on that one word: *seven*. After all, what else was there for me to say? And what could Mom say? What does a mother say to a daughter who has just told her she is expecting seven babies?

No sooner had I hung up the phone after talking to my mom than it rang. Kenny's stepmother, Val, had volunteered to drive me home from the hospital; she wanted to know what time she needed to come. I told her Dr. Emge had already released me. I should be ready to leave by the time she got to the hospital from Carlisle. Then Val asked how the ultrasound had gone.

"Fine," I told her.

"So, they found the baby?" she asked.

"Y-e-e-s-s."

She also read something in my voice. "Did they find more than one? How many?"

"Seven."

Funny how that one word could stop people in their tracks.

There was a short silence. "It'll be okay," Val reassured me. "I'll be right up."

While I waited for Val, a nurse came in to work on my hospital discharge paperwork. This nurse had taken care of me the day before and knew I had been downstairs for an ultrasound. As she stood in the doorway, making notes on my chart, she asked how the tests had gone.

"Did they find the baby?" she wanted to know.

"Yes," I told her. "All seven of them."

She looked up, a startled expression on her face for a fleeting moment. She set the chart down and walked slowly into the room.

"How far along did you say you were?"

"Five weeks."

"Don't panic yet," she told me. "Just because that's what they see on the ultrasound now doesn't mean that's what you'll end up with. They might have been counting empty sacs, sacs that never had anything in them to begin with. That often happens at this stage. Or, when all they can see is sacs, sometimes what they are seeing is the reflection of another sac.

"Even if there are seven babies now, you won't carry seven to full term. Nature has a way of taking care of this kind of situation. With this many you'll miscarry some of them and your body will just reabsorb the tissue—just as if they had not ever been there. You're probably going to end up with twins—maybe triplets, at most. There's a lot that can happen between now and your due date."

That made me feel a lot better. *This is going to be okay,* I thought. *There's no need to panic. Twins would be nice. I've been praying for twins. We could even handle triplets.*

Val arrived at the hospital and we headed for home. We made one stop at a drugstore to get a prescription. And we drove through Burger King to get something to eat. We arrived at the house just a few minutes before Kenny was due home for his lunch hour.

The one thought that had kept running through my mind for the past couple of hours, since the technician had pronounced the word *seven* for the first time, had been: *How am I going to tell Kenny?* I purposely hadn't called him yet. Kenny didn't need to hear about this while he was at work. I didn't know what his response would be, but I expected him to be upset about it at first. Kenny doesn't particularly like surprises. So I didn't want him to hear this news over the phone, in the office, in front of all his coworkers. I would never do that to him. I needed to tell him face-to-face.

But how? How do you gently break the news to your husband that you're pregnant with seven babies?

Kenny knew we were home when he saw Val's car in the driveway. The first words out of his mouth when he hurried through the kitchen door at the back of our home were, "How was the ultrasound? Did they find the baby?"

"Ye-e-e-s."

The expression on his face changed suddenly. He knew something was up.

"How many?" he asked.

"You'd better sit down," I told him.

"I don't want to sit down! How many?"

So I sat down. And I told him, "Seven."

It took a few moments to register. When it did, his first response was classic Kenny. He began pacing across the living room, down the short hallway by the bedrooms, and back again. At first he was muttering something unintelligible under his breath.

The faster and longer he paced the louder he got, until there was no mistaking his words. "No. NO. NO!" he was saying. "This is getting way out of hand!"

Val had stepped around the corner out of sight into the kitchen in order to cover her mouth and stifle her laughter. I could tell how upset Kenny was, so I didn't dare laugh. I knew he couldn't see any humor in the situation. At least not yet. But it was a pretty comical reaction.

This is getting way out of hand!

He made it sound as if I had just spent too much money at the mall. And I thought, *Well, it's not like I can return some babies and get my money back!*

So while Kenny paced and Val stayed hidden in the kitchen, listening and trying desperately to keep from laughing out loud, I waited. And watched my poor husband try to calm down enough to accept the biggest surprise of his life.

Kenny

I guess I pitched something of a tantrum when I heard the news. That word *seven* seemed unbelievable and overwhelming. My mind raced from one thought to another as I instantly began to consider the consequences, to think through the unthinkable. *How can we afford to have seven babies? Oh, man! How will we manage seven toddlers? Seven two-year-olds? Impossible! We'll never be able to send them all to college!*

Forget college! First things first. Where would seven babies sleep in this house? We don't have enough room!

Seven babies? This can't be happening! That means I'd be the father of eight children! I'm only twenty-seven years old! I'm too young to be the father of eight!

We had in just a few weeks gone from having one child, to hoping for another child, to the thrill of knowing that Bobbi was pregnant again, to the fear over the weekend that she was losing that baby in an ectopic pregnancy, and now to this unbelievable news. Seven babies? It was just too much to absorb.

There was no way that day, or for many months of days to come, that I could fully comprehend the implications of what I'd just heard. But from that moment when I heard Bobbi say the shocking word *seven* I did know one thing for certain: Life as I had known it had just ceased to exist.

Lord, I thought, *what is going on here? What are You doing to us?*

I continued to pace around the house for a while longer, until I finally settled down enough to eat. In fact, I ate both my lunch and Bobbi's, since she wasn't hungry. We talked some, although I don't remember much of what we said. I do remember Bobbi explaining what the nurse had told her—about the body reabsorbing some of the babies. That we couldn't possibly have seven.

Hearing that made me feel a little better. But what if we ended up with four or five babies? That thought was hardly reassuring. And if there were seven now, what if . . .

Oh, Lord, what is going on here?

Then, in what seemed like both an eternity and no time at all, it was time for me to go back to work.

I certainly wasn't ready to share my news with everyone else at work, but I wanted to tell my dad. I walked into the shop at the Chevy dealership, where Dad is a mechanic, and asked him to come with me. I led him back into one of the car stalls, behind a vehicle up on a hoist, where we would be out of the sight and hearing of his coworkers.

"Dad, I've got something to tell you," I began.

"What'd you find out?" he asked. "Is the baby okay?"

"Yeah. It's not the fact that there's one baby. We're having multiples."

Dad's eyes got big. "What? How many?"

"Seven."

A big smile spread across his face. "Shoo-o-o-e-e! Are you sure?"

"They counted seven sacs on the ultrasound today," I told him.

"Well, you guys will be able to handle it," he reassured me.

"We may not end up with seven babies," I explained to him. "There's a good chance that some of them will miscarry and just be reabsorbed into Bobbi's body. If it's not meant to be, God will use that natural process. Odds are we might see no more than four or five babies out of this."

Dad was still grinning and shaking his head.

Just having told my dad made me feel better. His matter-of-fact acceptance of our ability to handle whatever happened calmed me down a little. His obvious pleasure at the thought of all those grandbabies made me feel a little more positive myself. We both went back to work and finished out the afternoon.

When I got home that evening, I found out that Mikayla had gone over to my dad's house with Val, so that Bobbi and I could have some time alone. And our church, knowing that Bobbi had just gotten out of the hospital, had made arrangements for our supper. In fact our pastor and his wife, Ginny, brought over a turkey and stuffing dinner not long after I got home. They delivered the meal to our back door and then stood in the kitchen talking to us for a few minutes.

Pastor Brown carried his Bible under his arm as usual; he never goes anywhere without it. As we talked about our news, I admitted that I was worried. I had no idea how we could possibly afford seven babies. When I said that, Pastor opened his Bible and began to share verses with us. Two in particular stand out in my mind.

The first, Philippians 4:19, read: "My God shall supply all your need according to His riches in glory by Christ Jesus."

And 1 Corinthians 10:13, "No temptation has overtaken you except such as is common to man; but God is faithful, who will not allow you to be tempted above what you are able, but with the temptation will also make the way of escape, that you may be able to bear it."

As Pastor read those verses, I realized that Bobbi and I were not alone. That God would supply our needs, just as He always had. He would be faithful and make a way for us to handle whatever resulted from this pregnancy. If we could just leave it in His hands, everything would work out fine.

I really wanted to believe that. I could hear Pastor's words. I could even tell myself what he said was true. And that did help provide a small measure of peace.

But saying it and even knowing it were one thing. Believing it, really believing it, and feeling it were something else altogether.

Bobbi

After Pastor and Ginny left, we talked for a while. Kenny ate supper and I just picked at it, still not very hungry. Then we drove the block to Dad and Val's house to pick up Mikayla. When we got there Kenny headed down to the basement rec room with his dad, to play pool with his brother Matt and try to unwind. I sat in the kitchen and visited with Val about the day.

In the midst of all that had gone on, Mikayla hadn't taken her nap that afternoon. She was clearly tired and decided she wanted her mom. I remembered how she had clung to Kenny and refused to have anything to do with me in the hospital two days before. Now, she seemed to have forgiven me. She came over and lifted up her arms. I wanted to pick her up. But I couldn't, not so soon after surgery. So Mikayla leaned up against me and laid her head on my knee. I patted her head and stroked her hair. Within minutes she was fast asleep, head on my leg, standing up, propped between my knees there in the kitchen.

She looked so cute that Val called Kenny upstairs to see her. But by the time he got there, her legs had buckled. Kenny picked her up, and he and I took our sleeping daughter and headed home for the night.

Kenny

In bed that night Bobbi tried to read, as she does most nights. And I lay there, staring up at the ceiling, my thoughts spinning out of control again. *I still can't believe this. I just can't believe that this is happening to us. How are we going to do it? Seven! This is my worst nightmare coming true.*

When we turned out the light, tears came. We had really wanted another baby. Bobbi had actually prayed for twins. But seven! Not in our wildest dreams had we thought about seven babies. This was not what we had planned and not what we really wanted.

Bobbi

After we finished crying I lay awake for a while.

I was glad to be home in my own bed at last. I felt emotionally drained, but too exhausted to sleep. The news still seemed so unreal.

Seven babies? What if . . .

I worried about Mikayla. And I worried about Kenny.

He'd seemed a lot calmer this evening. But I realized he was still having a tough time dealing with this. Tougher than I was. I knew he wasn't a happy camper. *In fact, if this is true, our happy camping days may be over forever.*

Three

Blind Date Beginning

Kenny

*J*don't know that I'd say my entire life flashed before my eyes
as I tried to get to sleep that night. But my mind certainly
raced back and forth over the past as I attempted to make some
sense out of this new, sudden twist in our lives and also tried to
imagine what the future might now hold.

I remembered again the day Bobbi and I first met.

"Kenny, you have a phone call," my stepmom called through
the bathroom door. "It's Neil."

"Thanks, I'll take it in my room in just a minute."

After a hot afternoon on my summer job of washing cars at the
Wright Chevrolet dealership, I'd driven home and jumped in the
shower to clean up and cool down. Now I quickly finished dry-
ing off, wrapped the towel around me, and hurried to my room to
pick up the phone.

"Hey, Kenster! Got any plans tonight?"

"Not really," I told my buddy. "What's up?"

"A bunch of us are getting together to go bowling tonight. Wanna join us?"

"Okay," I replied. I didn't have anything better to do on that Friday night. "Do I need to pick anyone up?"

"Nah," he told me. "We're going to the Fairlanes at Euclid and 14th. Just meet us there in an hour."

I knew the place—on the north side of Des Moines. I knew Neil better. We'd been friends four or five years. He and I had met when I was sixteen or seventeen and our neighboring church youth groups competed against each other in Bible quizzing contests at Christian youth rallies conducted around the state of Iowa. During the past couple of years we'd become even closer friends as fellow classmates at Faith Baptist Bible College in nearby Ankeny, Iowa.

He'd become a youth leader for his church, so I naturally assumed that the "bunch of us" going bowling would include teenagers from his youth group and maybe even some mutual college friends.

I pulled into the bowling alley's parking lot a little early and sat waiting in my car for Neil and his crowd to arrive. A few minutes later I saw him turn in. I recognized Barbara sitting beside him in the passenger seat; she was his steady girlfriend and also a student at Faith. I couldn't tell who was sitting in the backseat.

By the time I'd climbed out of my car Neil was walking toward me with Barbara and another girl I'd never seen before. "Where's the rest of the group?" I asked as they drew near.

Neil and Barbara both laughed. "This is it," Neil said.

"You're kidding," I said. "What is this? A blind date or something?"

"Yup!" Neil grinned.

"Kenny," Barbara said, "I'd like you to meet my sister Bobbi."

As surprised as I was, Bobbi obviously felt even more awkward.

Bobbi

I was mortified.

When I'd gotten off work at a local bridal shop, Barbara had told me, "Some of us are going bowling tonight, why don't you come along?"

I should have suspected something was up when I told her I'd be ready to go as soon as I changed into more casual clothes, because she'd said, "Don't change. What you have on will be fine."

I started to protest, "I think I'll be more comfortable in . . ."

"Trust me," Barbara had said. "You don't want to change."

Still, it wasn't until we pulled into the bowling alley parking lot and I heard Barbara tell Neil, "There's his car," that everything suddenly dawned on me.

"I don't believe this!" I told my sister. "You are dead, Barbara!" I think Neil laughed. Barbara knew better. But there was no gracious way out. I had no choice but to go through with what promised to be a terribly awkward evening.

I assumed Kenny felt as embarrassed as I did. He spent most of our time in the bowling alley talking to Neil, leaving me to converse with my scheming sister.

I did keep a close eye on Kenny, however. A shot-putter and discus thrower back in high school, he'd taken up weight lifting during his college days and was really built. I remember thinking, *He's so handsome he's never even going to notice me.*

After bowling the four of us went to a nearby pizza place where Barbara and Neil managed to slip into one side of the booth, leaving Kenny and me no choice but to scoot in next to each other. Barbara and Neil still carried most of the conversation, but we all talked a little more as we ate.

From there we went to the Scott Street bridge where all four of us walked out on an old railroad trestle over the Des Moines River and sat for a while in the dark enjoying the starry night and more conversation. By this time I'd realized that despite his macho good looks, there was also a kind of gentle, honest, vulnerability about Kenny that really appealed to me. He even had nice manners. I was thinking maybe I wouldn't strangle my sister when we got home after all. *I could like this guy . . . but who am I kidding? He's so good-looking I will probably never hear from him again.*

I don't remember how we got on the subject; Barbara and Neil probably steered the conversation toward the topic of dating. That's how I learned Kenny had fairly recently broken up with a girl he'd been dating a while. It was in that context Kenny admitted he had begun to wonder if maybe the Lord might be calling him to be single "like He did the apostle Paul."

When he said that I thought, *Oh no! Who wants to be single?*

A little later, when I learned he was only twenty-one, I wondered how he'd react when he learned I'd just turned twenty-three. For some guys the fact I was almost two years older could be a major turnoff. It was looking more and more as though the evening would be a total waste.

As reluctant as I was to get my hopes up, when Barbara and I got home that evening I asked her if she thought Neil could arrange another date. Realizing I'd forgiven her for the blind date, she grinned and shook her head. "I think Neil's done all the matchmaking he's going to do. If Kenny wants to see you again, he'll give you a call."

A few days later Kenny phoned to ask if he could come over. I said, "Sure." And when he did, we talked for a while before he asked me out for the coming Friday night.

On our first real date we ate at a very nice, moderately priced restaurant. Then he took me back to his house where I met his family and we all watched the movie-video *Dances with Wolves* while we had soft drinks and munched on popcorn.

From the very beginning our dating life revolved around family—and church. We double-dated quite a bit with Barbara and Neil. The first time we kissed was at church one Sunday evening after a regular youth group get-together ironically referred to as SNOOP—Sunday Night Occurrence of Pleasure. We were sitting and talking in his car in the Missionary Baptist Church parking lot when he asked permission to kiss me.

I thought that was so romantic! Not the church parking lot, but his asking. After knowing him only a month, I knew I was crazy about the guy.

Kenny

By the end of our fateful blind date I remember thinking, *Wow! This is a real possibility!* When I got home that night, I told my stepmom how Neil and Barbara had set up the whole thing. Val laughed and asked how it went. I told her a little about Bobbi and admitted, "I really like her."

Before long Bobbi and I became such a regular item that most of my buddies began giving me a hard time: "Hey, Kenster! Weren't you the guy who swore off serious relationships? What about that 'single life' calling you used to talk about?"

I didn't care what anyone else said or thought. I was fast falling in love. I wanted to spend as much time as possible with Bobbi, learning everything there was to know about her.

Bobbi told me she was the oldest of six children in her family. She'd been born in Alberta, Canada, where her parents, Bob and Peggy Hepworth, met while attending school at Prairie Bible Institute. Her sister Barbara, whom I'd met first, was just twelve days short of a year younger than Bobbi. Their brother Pete came along a year or so later.

The Hepworths added Bill to their family when Bobbi was eight years old. A year and a half later, her sister Michele entered the world. And at the time we started dating, her youngest sibling, Dennis, was only six years old, seventeen years younger than Bobbi.

"People used to look at our big family and ask Dad if he was Mormon," Bobbi said. "When he'd tell them he wasn't, they would say, 'Then you must be crazy.' As if those were the only two explanations they could imagine."

Bob Hepworth, a Baptist minister, pastored churches in Michigan, Iowa, Kansas, and New Mexico. According to Bobbi, moving as much as they did was tough. So were the high expectations imposed on preachers' kids. Add to that all the responsibility that just naturally falls to the oldest child in a large family and it wasn't surprising that family always seemed so important to Bobbi.

When she was twelve Bobbi's father left full-time ministry and moved the family back to his roots in the small central Michigan town of Owosso. That's where Bobbi spent her teenage years and her dad began a new career servicing medical equipment (such as X-ray and ultrasound machines) for hospitals, clinics, and doctors' and dentists' offices around the state.

Because Bobbi had grown up in a strong Christian home as a minister's daughter, faith played a crucial part in her life from the beginning. But the Bible and Christian beliefs weren't just abstract things her parents taught. She made her own personal decision for Christ as a five-year-old when a teacher prayed with her between Sunday school and church one Sunday morning. And it was that lasting, personal commitment, plus a desire for a deeper understanding of her own faith, that led Bobbi to follow in her parents' footsteps after high school and enroll at Prairie Bible Institute.

By the time Bobbi completed two years of Bible school in Canada, her dad had tired of Michigan winters and decided to move the family to Las Vegas, Nevada. Bobbi rejoined her family there, finding employment as a salesclerk at a small lace and fabric shop across town from the Strip.

When I expressed surprise that a Baptist minister's daughter would live in Las Vegas of all places, Bobbi shrugged off the irony. "If you're not into the gambling scene, it's really a lot like living anywhere else," she insisted. "With the exception that you have a few more options to choose from if you wake up at 1:00 A.M. and decide you want to go out to eat."

The reason Bobbi ended up in Iowa goes back to her sister. Barbara had followed Bobbi to Prairie Bible Institute. While there Barbara made a trip to Des Moines to visit their maternal grandmother. In the process she had met Neil and suddenly felt "led" to transfer to Faith Baptist Bible College for a semester "to be near Grandma"—at least that's what she told her folks. That's where I met Barbara, and, I found out later, that's when she began writing and trying to convince Bobbi to come to Iowa. "There are a lot more eligible Christian guys here than in Las Vegas," she said. "In fact, Neil has a couple of friends who might be good candidates."

Bobbi moved to Des Moines in the spring of 1991. She lived with her sister and soon landed a job as a salesclerk/seamstress at a dress shop called "The Bridal Connection." It took another four months before Neil and Barbara engineered our first date. But once they did, I was ready to take it from there.

Before I met Bobbi I'd come up with a checklist of things I felt would be necessary in any woman I ever considered marrying—that was *if* I did consider marriage and didn't stay single all my life. Looking back, my "ideal woman" qualifications seem rather limited and perhaps more than a little naive. But I was very serious about it at the time.

Being a typical male, the first thing on my checklist was that she "has to be pretty." But in my own defense, I was concerned about a lot more than good looks. Most important, I knew I would need someone who shared my personal faith, a deeply committed Christian who had a genuine, personal faith of her own. I also wanted to find someone who had grown up with a strong Christian home background—someone who would be committed to having a Christian family and for whom family relationships and values would be an important priority.

Bobbi met all these criteria and more. As the oldest of six children she had lots of experience caring for younger siblings. She seemed such an emotionally even-keeled person, so calm, so capable and practical, that I knew she'd make a great mother—if we ever had children. And when she and Barbara would invite Neil and me to eat supper at the little rental house they shared, I learned Bobbi was also a terrific cook. What more could a guy ask for?

Bobbi

Some women might have been put off by Kenny's checklist of what he was looking for in a wife. I took it as encouraging proof that he saw marriage as a very important commitment deserving of serious thought. And the more I learned about Kenny, the better I understood his reasoning.

His parents, Ken McCaughey and Kathy Smith, had married young. They had Kenny right away and five years later Kenny's brother Jason. The family bought a home and lived in Hartford, Iowa, a smaller town just down the road and a few cornfields southeast of Carlisle, where Ken landed a job as a mechanic for Wright Chevrolet.

When Ken and Kathy divorced a few years later, Kenny had to make a decision no seven-year-old should ever have to face. He loved both his parents, but he had to choose which one he wanted to live with. He and his brother went with his mom when she moved first to Indianola, ten miles away, and eventually to Columbus Junction, which was a three-hour drive from Des Moines. Yet many of Kenny's roots and a big part of his heart remained with his dad in Hartford and in Carlisle where Ken worked. Kenny had made lots of friends while attending kindergarten and first and second grades at Carlisle Elementary School. He came back "home" often, to visit his father on weekends, holidays, and during summer vacations.

Ken McCaughey married Val Templeton in 1980 when Kenny was ten years old. It wasn't long before the two of them started a family; first Kenny had a new little brother named Matt, then a baby sister by the name of Alisha.

Those weren't the only changes that took place in his father's life. Through the influence of friends they used to party with, Ken and Val became involved in a local church and were, as we Baptists say, "saved." Kenny recognized a huge difference when he'd come to visit Ken and Val. Not only had his dad and his stepmom drastically changed their lifestyle—giving up partying, smoking, and drinking—but Kenny also sensed a new peace and contentment about his father. Even Ken's language changed. He and Val became churchgoers for the first time in their lives.

Kenny was impressed by the difference he saw in his father and stepmother when he stayed with them the summer he was sixteen. He began attending church with them and heard the gospel message for the first time. Before that summer ended Kenny made his own decision to accept Jesus Christ as his Savior, joined Carlisle's Missionary Baptist Church, and decided that he wanted to try living with his father again.

Kenny broke the news of his decision to his mom as gently as he knew how. He explained his decision to live a Christian life and told her that to do that he thought he needed a different home environment and a strong church influence. He knew his mom felt hurt when he left, but within a couple of years, after seeing the difference Kenny's faith had made in his life, his mom, too, had a conversion experience. Today both Kenny's dad and Val, and Kathy and her husband, Dave Addleman, are committed Christians, with strong personal faiths and regular involvement in their own churches. "It's made a real difference in all our relationships," Kenny told me.

Affected by the impact their newfound faith had on his entire family and convinced of its importance in his own life, Kenny determined the first step in the rest of his life would be to try to gain a better understanding of those beliefs. When he graduated from Carlisle High School in 1988, he enrolled at nearby Faith Baptist Bible College.

After two years at Faith he transferred most of his credits to Des Moines Area Community College on the north side of the city. He was a DMACC student when I met him, working toward an Associate of Arts degree in business administration and not at all sure what he was going to do next.

Kenny

It didn't take me long to decide that whatever the future held, I wanted to share it all with Bobbi Hepworth. She soon let me know she felt the same way about me.

By Christmas of 1991 we'd discussed marriage and talked about becoming officially engaged that next summer when I finished school. If everything went as planned, we figured we'd have the wedding the following December. By the first of the year we even went to jewelry stores to look at wedding rings because Bobbi wanted to make sure I knew what she wanted. She was particular, not about size but about style.

I still managed to surprise her by moving up the timetable. On April 19, 1992, the day after Neil and Barbara's wedding, I drove Bobbi out to Lake Ahquabi, one of our favorite scenic destinations. We parked near a spot where a couple of months before we'd carved our initials in an old dead tree stump at the edge of a woods—not far from the road.

"Let's see if they are still there," I suggested. So we set out on a short hike. When we found the stump, and our initials, I took Bobbi's hands, knelt on the ground, and asked, "Will you marry me?"

Bobbi knew I'd already asked for and received her father's permission when he'd come to Iowa for Neil and Barbara's wedding. But this still caught her completely off guard.

"Would you please get up?" she asked, obviously embarrassed and quickly looking around to see how many other people in the park might be watching us. I could have taken offense if I hadn't already learned how much Bobbi hated to be the center of attention. "Just get up," she pleaded as I hesitated.

"Not until you answer my question," I told her.

"Yes! Yes, I'll marry you. Now get up!"

Her response wasn't quite as warm and romantic as I'd expected. It did get me on my feet where I really surprised her by pulling out the ring.

That's when she seemed to forget all about anyone watching as she slipped the ring on and gave me a big hug and kiss. This was a little more the reaction I'd been expecting.

Bobbi

The worst part of Kenny's proposal wasn't the awkwardness I felt when he got down on his knees like that out in public. It was the fact that Barbara and Neil were on their honeymoon and the rest of my family were all on the road home after the wedding. I couldn't call anyone in my family to share the exciting news.

Not that we needed to be in a big rush. We'd already decided that December 5 would be a workable date for my family in Las Vegas and other relatives in Michigan to come back to Iowa for another wedding. Almost eight months away, our wedding date gave everyone a chance to plan and provided us more than enough time to talk about and anticipate not just our wedding, but our marriage.

I vividly recall our first serious discussion about children. When I told Kenny I wanted to have six kids we were eating hamburgers at Burger King. He nearly fell out of his seat!

I don't think he believed me.

I assured him I was serious. I enjoyed growing up in a big family and had always wanted a big family of my own. This may seem a little old-fashioned, perhaps even politically incorrect to admit, but I had always dreamed of growing up to be a mother and wife with a big family, a loving husband, and a life to live happily ever after. I knew a lot of people who probably thought I should have had higher aspirations. But I didn't think there was a higher or more important calling to aspire to than mothering.

Kenny said when he thought of getting married he'd always imagined a family someday. But he was thinking more in terms of *two* children, "maybe three." And "not for a while," because he didn't think he was quite ready for the kind of responsibility that comes with parenthood.

We obviously had some differing expectations to work through when it came to our family. I think we both knew that. But, we told ourselves, *We have time to work this out. After all, we're in love!*

Kenny

I didn't think December 5 would ever come. But it did. And since her family had no long-term church roots in Las Vegas, Bobbi and I were married in my home church in Carlisle. We'd attended Missionary Baptist together during our courting days. We both now intended to make it our own church home.

Bobbi planned a very traditional wedding. Her father conducted the service. Since we both enjoy music, we talked about singing one of the songs together during the service, but we decided we would probably be too nervous. So we recorded the number ahead of time and played it as part of the ceremony—during the lighting of the unity candle just before we were pronounced husband and wife. The words of the song *Household of Faith*, which we'd heard on an album by contemporary Christian music artist Steve Green, summed up the testimony we wanted to declare to our friends and relatives:

Here we are at the start committing to each other
By His Word and from our hearts
We will be a family in a house that will be a home
And with faith we'll build it strong.

We'll build a household of faith
That together we can make
And when the strong winds blow it won't fall down
As one in Him we'll grow and the whole world will know
That we are a household of faith.

Now to be a family, we've got to love each other
At any cost unselfishly.
And our home must be a place that fully abounds with grace
A reflection of His face.

We'll build a household of faith
That together we can make
And when the strong winds blow it won't fall down
As one in Him we'll grow and the whole world will know
That we are a household of faith.

The entire song held special meaning for us, but it was those
last words of the chorus we sang that spelled out the central goal
Bobbi and I wished to set for our marriage and life together. So:
 . . . *the whole world will know that we are a household of*
faith.

Four

Will We Ever Have Kids?

Bobbi

Our courtship continued right on into those early days of our marriage. We had adjustments to make, of course. After living on my own for years, being independent, and making my own decisions, it took me a while to get used to discussing and deciding things as a couple. I had to learn to respect and value the opinions and wishes of someone who didn't always think or react to things the way I did.

We both came into marriage with our own expectations based on our very different upbringings and personalities. We endured our share of misunderstandings and silly arguments over the most petty things. I remember one blowup we had over goulash; I fixed it with canned tomatoes and Kenny preferred using spaghetti sauce instead.

But we survived the adjustments. And we reached our first anniversary more in love than ever.

Kenny

We lived in an apartment complex right in Carlisle, close enough for me to walk to work at Wright Chevrolet. At the time we got married I worked detailing cars in the service department. Bobbi continued her job at the Bridal Connection, though she worked less as a salesclerk and more as a seamstress, not only doing all the alterations but also cutting out, assembling, and sewing the store's popular new line of Budget Bride bridesmaids' dresses.

While neither of us made a lot of money in our jobs, we did have a very real financial goal. By working hard and being especially frugal we wanted to save, as soon as possible, enough money for a down payment on a house.

We planned to start our family within a couple of years. And by the time our first child was born, we wanted a house to raise him or her in.

We began exploring the housing market in Des Moines itself. Since real estate prices are lower there than in Carlisle, we thought we'd be more likely to find something in our price range in the city.

Still, we never quite gave up the dream of living in Carlisle. Not only was it home for me, but we both valued the small town atmosphere. Neighbors were friends and friends were neighbors there. My work was there. So was our church. And my family still lived just down the road in neighboring Hartford.

When the For Sale sign went up in front of a little place on First Street, just six short blocks from the middle of town and an eight- to ten-minute walk from Wright Chevrolet, I immediately called to ask about it. We knew the place was small (less than 800 square feet), so we were surprised to learn it had three bedrooms. We figured those bedrooms had to be tiny. And they were—the third one much better suited to be a sewing room for Bobbi than a bedroom. The place needed some cosmetic work, but we were more than willing to do the necessary fix-up to obtain such a livable house.

In September of 1994 we moved into a home we could afford, a home that would meet our needs, in the very town where we wanted to live and raise our family. We'd been married twenty-one months and all our plans seemed to be right on schedule. Except for one thing.

We hadn't yet started the family we wanted to raise in our new house.

Bobbi

I'd have been happy to get pregnant on our honeymoon. I wanted a big family and I was already twenty-four and a half years old. I could almost hear my biological clock ticking.

Kenny still thought we ought to wait to have children. So we agreed the ideal compromise would be to get pregnant after the first year and have our first baby just before our second anniversary—right about the time we purchased our first home.

So the fact that we weren't even pregnant when we moved in was a major discouragement for me—and I'd already been discouraged for months.

In the fall of 1993, nearly a year after our wedding, I went in for an appointment with my obstetrician/gynecologist. I talked to him about wanting to start a family. After he conducted an exam and took a detailed history he told me he didn't think I was ovulating on my own. If we wanted to begin our family right away he suggested I begin charting my basal body temperature to determine if and when I ovulated. Plus he thought I should simultaneously begin taking a small dose of Clomid in the hopes that the most common of fertility drugs would regulate my very irregular cycle by triggering a normal monthly ovulation.

Feeling encouraged by my doctor's optimism, I took one dose of Clomid a day for five days the next time I had my period. And I told my family, "This time next month we should be pregnant!"

It didn't happen.

The next time the doctor prescribed two Clomid a day for five days. I just knew we'd get pregnant over our first wedding anniversary.

We didn't. And what was more discouraging was the doctor's conclusion that I still wasn't ovulating.

We tried three Clomid a day for five days. No success. The doctor upped it to four a day, then five a day.

Since my periods were so irregular, each month that I took Clomid I would reach that fourteenth day after ovulation and think I was pregnant. I would get a home pregnancy kit and take the test while no one else was around. When the results were negative, I would cry.

The psychological letdown was huge—and horrible.

One month I started the test just before my sister Barbara called to chat. I should have waited until we were off the phone to check the results. But I didn't. I carried the phone with me to look at the test. It was negative, again. I never did let on to Barbara. But when that phone call ended, I sat at my sewing machine, sewing and crying my eyes out, for the rest of the morning.

I told Kenny I didn't know how many times I could endure this emotional roller coaster of rising hopes and crashing disappointment. I wasn't sure Kenny could really empathize. His attitude seemed to be more accepting: Whatever God gives us (or doesn't give us) we should accept as His will. If we never have any children, so be it.

For me it wasn't that simple. Every time we failed to get pregnant I grieved for the child we couldn't have. I struggled with a very real, very deep sense of loss.

Cost was another factor in the equation. At ten dollars a pop, Clomid seemed relatively inexpensive at the outset. Just fifty dollars the first month. The cost doubled for the second round and tripled for the third. By the time we worked up to five doses a day for five days (which we did twice), we were talking about a substantial chunk out of our meager monthly budget. All for nothing—or almost nothing.

Those last two cycles the doctor did decide I ovulated. Yet he didn't know why I'd not gotten pregnant. He suggested it was time to see a fertility specialist and pursue other options.

With my irregular cycle, the six rounds of Clomid had taken nearly eighteen months. By this time we'd begun 1995 and didn't seem any closer to needing that second bedroom of the new house we'd lived in for almost six months. We'd obviously trashed the original timetable we'd had for starting a family. I could only pray that my lifelong dreams of motherhood wouldn't be shattered as well.

Kenny

The longer we went without getting pregnant, and the more Bobbi read and told me about alternative fertility treatments, the more I wondered: *What are we getting into here? How far are we willing to take this? Maybe we should simply trust God and let nature take its course. In tampering with nature are we "playing God"? What if it is God's will that Bobbi and I not have children?*

I saw how devastated Bobbi was every month we weren't pregnant. I knew how desperately she wanted children. So I didn't share all my questions with her. But I did ask them of myself.

Bobbi's OB recommended a couple of fertility specialists practicing in Des Moines. That's when we first heard of Dr. Katherine Hauser. But our insurance didn't include her on their list of providers, so we opted for someone who was.

Bobbi made her first appointment with Dr. Donald Young in February of 1995. He told Bobbi what she already knew: that there were often more than one interrelated, complicating factor contributing to a couple's fertility problems. That meant there was a variety of treatments with which to address the problem. After running a simple HSG test to make certain Bobbi's fallopian tubes were not blocked (they weren't), Dr. Young suggested that since Clomid hadn't worked for us, we should consider a more powerful but more effective drug called Perganol.

I had my doubts when Bobbi came home to tell me about her appointment. I still wasn't sure how far we should take this whole business of infertility treatment.

But Bobbi explained that Perganol, like Clomid, simply provided natural hormones her body for some reason didn't produce enough of. The use of Perganol involved two complementary hormones that worked together to give an extra boost of stimulation to the ovaries to produce eggs.

Unlike in vitro fertilization and other more extreme or invasive procedures she admitted she, too, had questions about, Bobbi had no hesitation whatsoever about using these common fertility drugs. As she explained, "We're just using normal human hormones to help the natural, God-given process work the way He intended."

When I thought about it in that way I realized we were no more "playing God" than a person plays God by taking insulin or thyroid supplements. Or the millions of women who take estrogen in some form every day.

Our only goal was to try to get Bobbi's body to work the way God designed human bodies to work.

That explanation answered my questions once and for all. We had an easy decision to make. If Clomid hadn't worked, the next logical and obvious step was Perganol.

Bobbi called the doctor's office to set up a time for us to go in for training. Unlike Clomid, which came in pill form, Perganol had to be injected. And I was the one who would give Bobbi her shots—once a day for eight days.

The nurse who instructed us walked into the room carrying a needle and syringe along with one of those foam rubber insulation sleeves people slip over drink cans to keep the contents cold. "You can practice on this," she told us. "We think this foam rubber simulates the texture and resistance of human skin better than anything else we've found."

I decided to clown around and tossed the needled syringe like a dart at the cup holder. Bobbi was not amused. For some reason she didn't like the idea of me using her backside as a dartboard.

The nurse thought I was funnier than Bobbi did. "We find that a lot of men can't deal with giving shots—especially with the size of needle we need for an intramuscular injection like this. So a certain number of our women patients have to inject themselves. Perhaps you'll want to consider that option," she told Bobbi.

Suddenly feeling my masculine pride at stake, I assured the

nurse, "I'm very sure that won't be necessary for us." And it wasn't.

We did encounter an unexpected problem when we called to let the fertility doctor's office know Bobbi had started her next period. "I'm afraid there's bad news," we were told. "We're completely out of Perganol and our supplier says there won't be any available for a while. They recommend an improved version of Perganol called Metrodin. It works the same way—only better—according to the company that makes both drugs. So you have a choice. We can use Metrodin or we can wait and see when we might get a new shipment of Perganol."

We opted to use Metrodin. Starting on the third day of Bobbi's period I began injecting two amps a day for seven days and one more amp of the drug on the eighth day. Bobbi went in for ultrasounds of her ovaries on the first, third, fifth, sixth, seventh, and eighth days to look for mature follicles. Finally, on the eighth day, the doctor found three eggs that were large enough, 20 mm across, to be considered "ripe."

He gave Bobbi the additional hormone HCG, which triggers the release of the follicle and, thirty-six hours later, a syringeful of my sperm was injected into Bobbi's uterus close to the fallopian tubes. Then we had to wait once again for the results.

Bobbi

On the whole, fertility treatments themselves weren't that bad—even the shots. But as I'd learned while taking Clomid, the waiting was agony.

I felt different this time. The treatment left me feeling really full, as if I'd eaten way too much food at a potluck dinner. I got sick each morning—which I took as an encouraging sign. On the morning of the twelfth day following the insemination I went back to the doctor's office for a blood test wanting desperately to believe it would come back positive.

I spent the rest of that day at Barbara and Neil's house because I didn't want to wait alone. Our younger sister, Michele, was also visiting Barbara that day.

I planned to call for the results as soon as my brother-in-law left for work that afternoon. But Neil wouldn't leave; he kept hanging around—clearly wanting to hear my news.

Finally he pulled Barbara aside and asked, "Why doesn't Bobbi call the doctor?"

My sister, who knows me as well as anyone else in the world, told him, "I think she's waiting for you to leave; she probably doesn't want to break down and cry in front of you if it's bad news."

Neil, who can sometimes take a hint, did. I'm not sure he'd even backed out of the driveway before I picked up the phone and dialed the doctor's office to hear four of the most wonderful words I'd ever heard in my life: "*The test was positive.* Congratulations, Mrs. McCaughey!"

"We're pregnant!" I told my husband when he answered his phone.

"No kidding?! We're pregnant!" he echoed the announcement to his entire office. I could hear the cheers and applause in the background.

"We're pregnant!" I practically shouted at my sisters in the next room. The three of us hugged and cried.

Two weeks later, the day before Easter, Barbara and I were together again when she pulled me into a back room of the house to say, "I've got something to tell you, Bobbi. I've been praying so hard that you would be pregnant, because I found out last month we are expecting again." (She and Neil already had a fourteen-month-old son, Zachary.) "And I didn't want to go through this pregnancy being happy when you couldn't be. But now we can enjoy our pregnancies together."

We both cried and hugged again.

Kenny

I never imagined how excited I'd be until I heard those words, "We're pregnant!" It was finally true. *I'm gonna be a father. No, anyone can be a father just like anyone can change a diaper. I want to be a dad!*

I couldn't stop grinning the rest of the day.

I'm not sure I quit grinning for the next nine months. I got a special kick out of imagining my own dad as a grandpa. He grinned a lot, too, because this was going to be the very first grandchild on my side of the family.

I'd never seen Bobbi so happy or so excited. As hard as it was to get pregnant, being pregnant turned out to be a breeze. For me at least.

Bobbi spotted a little blood very early in the pregnancy, but the doctor did an ultrasound to make sure everything looked fine. He assured us a little bleeding was a common enough occurrence at the time of implantation. Bobbi experienced some morning sickness the first three or four months. But even that was minor; she never threw up.

Our due date fell just five days before Christmas. We prayed for an early delivery so we could celebrate the holidays as a family. Instead, our first child decided to arrive very, very late.

Dr. Emge, our obstetrician, set January 3 as the date we would need to induce. But Bobbi woke me up that morning saying, "I think you better drive me to the hospital. I'm already in labor."

We jumped in the car and began timing contractions on the way. Regular. Five minutes apart.

I made a quick stop at a convenience store and spilled scalding coffee all over the front of my shirt as we pulled away. Maybe I wasn't as ready for parenthood as I'd thought.

Bobbi

It discouraged me to get to the hospital with strong contractions three minutes apart and be told I was only three centimeters dilated. I wanted to have my baby right then; but it would be another six hours before the doctor told me I could start pushing.

Those may well have been the longest six hours in our marriage. Labor progressed far too slowly to keep Kenny focused. He clicked through channels on the labor room's TV remote as if there were no tomorrow. I got so irritated I nearly bit his head off. "Pick a channel and leave it!" I told him.

Then he began calling everyone he knew and I suspected a few people he didn't. When he finally hung up the phone momentarily I told him, "Don't pick that up again!"

"What do you expect me to do in here?" he complained.

"How about coming over here and holding my hand?"

"Okay," he agreed. But a few moments later he tried to kiss me.

"Don't try to touch me!" I told him. "Just sit here quietly and hold my hand."

That lasted for a while—until the contractions intensified and I had to breathe through each one to maintain control.

"Don't push!" Kenny instructed. "Don't push!"

"I'm *not* going to push!" I told him. "Just be quiet."

At another point when I moaned loudly Kenny suggested that I "keep it a little quieter. They can hear you in the next room."

That's when I felt like kicking him—into the next room. But just about the time I decided I'd rather have this baby without him, I felt the first urge to push. "Aaaah! I can't do this!" I exclaimed as that contraction peaked and finally subsided.

And just like an experienced professional birthing coach, Kenny remembered exactly what he needed to say. "Yes you can!" he insisted. And he kept telling me that over and over until our baby was finally born.

"It's a girl!" he declared. "Mikayla Marie!"

I began weeping with joy. We'd prayed for a girl. A brown-eyed, red-haired girl. We'd gotten just what we'd prayed for. Her charm was a bonus—something Mikayla and God provided all on their own.

I enjoyed Kenny's reaction to our daughter immensely. The first time I saw my big, strong husband cradling that tiny bundle in his arms I knew he was in love. And so was I—with both of them.

But I soon learned Kenny lacked even more in childcare experience than he did in labor coaching techniques. Mikayla was about ten weeks old when I made an appointment to have my hair done while Kenny baby-sat.

Just minutes after I arrived at the beauty shop the phone rang: "It's for a Mrs. McCaughey."

"That's me."

I took the phone. Kenny was frantic. "The baby's crying and she won't stop. You have to come home!"

"I can't come home. I'm halfway through a perm."

"You've got to come home *now*! She won't stop crying!"

"Did you change her diaper?"

"Yeah!"

"Did you try giving her a bottle?"

"She won't take a bottle. She screams when I try to give it to her."

"She will take a bottle. You just have to calm her down."

"She won't quit screaming. You gotta come home."

"I can't come home until I'm finished here, Kenny. You'll just have to take care of Mikayla yourself."

When I got home an hour or so later, Kenny's dad and his twelve-year-old sister, Alisha, were there. Kenny had called in reinforcements. He needed two extra people to help him cope with one crying baby.

I had to laugh. Kenny didn't think it funny at all.

Kenny

I will admit I had a lot to learn about babies. But Mikayla turned out to be a great motivator. Because we took her everywhere with us, she didn't change our lifestyle nearly as much as I'd expected.

My daughter did, however, change my attitude about parenthood. I loved that little girl so much, I decided a big family wouldn't be an unpleasant proposition after all. While I don't remember admitting it out loud to Bobbi, I could see the appeal of three, four, maybe even five more like Mikayla.

So when Bobbi talked about wanting to have a second child close enough in age to Mikayla that they could be playmates and good friends, I was certainly agreeable. Unfortunately Bobbi's cycles continued to be irregular; Mikayla turned one without us getting pregnant again.

We were willing to consider Metrodin a second time. It had

worked wonders before. But we'd changed health insurance companies recently and didn't think we'd be able to afford to pay the portion of the treatment our new plan wouldn't cover. The cost of a single course of Metrodin, including doctor visits, medicine, lab tests, and ultrasounds added up to $2,500.

One day my stepmother, Val, came to see us. "Your dad and I have been talking," she told us. "We know you've been wanting another child right away. We've also heard you say you don't think you can afford the treatments right now. We've decided to loan you the thousand dollars your insurance won't pay. That way you can get started on your family right away and just pay us back when you can."

We accepted the generous offer. Bobbi made an appointment with Dr. Katherine Hauser, who was a provider for our new insurance. She took our history, learned that Metrodin had worked before, and recommended we give it a second try.

The next time Bobbi had her period we started the very same procedure we had followed with Mikayla. We injected the same dosage of Metrodin for the same eight days. The ultrasound showed the same results—three mature follicles ready for release.

The entire procedure was a carbon copy of our first experience. We had every reason to expect the same results. And another little girl just like Mikayla would have been fine with us. After all, you can't improve on perfection.

Bobbi

Twelve days after insemination I went in for my blood test. "Check back with us after four this afternoon for the results," the nurse told me.

At 4:01 that afternoon I called Dr. Hauser's office. When the

receptionist answered I identified myself and told her I was calling for the results of a pregnancy test conducted that morning.

"I'm sorry, Mrs. McCaughey," she said. "I don't believe we've
received those lab reports yet."

"The nurse told me to call after four," I informed her.

"Let me check then," she said, and the phone went dead for a
minute or so before she came back on. "Mrs. McCaughey?"

"Yes?" I responded.

"We did just get the lab results in. Your test was positive.
Congratulations!"

I felt like screaming with joy. Instead, I thanked the woman as
calmly as possible and simply hung up. *We're pregnant again!
Mikayla's going to be a big sister! I've got to call Kenny!*

I immediately dialed the dealership and asked for my husband.
The moment he picked up the line I told him, "I just got off the
phone with the doctor's office."

"What'd they say?" he wanted to know.

"We're pregnant!"

"Awright!" Kenny exclaimed. Then his voice became muted as
he turned his head and announced to his whole office: "We're
pregnant again!"

I could hear the spontaneous cheers and applause in the background before Kenny came back on to say, "That's great news!
What's the due date?"

"I haven't tried to figure it out yet. Sometime toward the end
of January next year," I said after quickly counting months on my
fingers.

"Who else knows?" Kenny asked.

"I called you first," I told him. *Who do you think I'd call?*

But I did dial my mom and Barbara as soon as I hung up the
phone after talking to Kenny. "We're pregnant!" I announced

each time. They both had pretty much the same reaction— pleased but hardly surprised. "We knew you would be. We've been praying."

I remember thinking, *I guess that's the downside of having so many folks praying. It's hard to surprise people who are praying expectantly.*

But my family certainly didn't anticipate the way their prayers would be answered this time. And neither did anyone else.

Five

Seven Heartbeats, Seven Babies

Bobbi

*J*have reviewed the ultrasounds we did at the time of your fertility treatment," Dr. Katherine Hauser, our fertility specialist, told me. "I simply do not see how you can be carrying seven fetuses." Dr. Hauser's phone call came on Friday, May 30. I had been at home for just over two days, recuperating from surgery and trying to comprehend the possibility of seven babies.

After Dr. Hauser had received the reports from Dr. Emge and Lutheran Hospital, she was concerned about how I was doing. So she'd phoned and we talked for almost half an hour. She discussed a number of things, some of which I already knew but were reassuring nonetheless.

During fertility treatment, especially when taking the medication Metrodin, ultrasounds are done at the time of ovulation to determine the number of mature follicles, or eggs ready to be fertilized. If too many follicles had been ripe, we would have had to wait another month to try to get pregnant.

But, at the time I had ovulated, only three ripe follicles had been visible on the ultrasound. Three mature eggs is considered an ideal number. Ordinarily, doctors expect only one or, possibly, two out of three to be fertilized and then successfully implanted in the uterus. Three had given us a good chance at getting pregnant without running the risk of a large multiple birth.

Dr. Hauser had been looking at those ultrasounds, taken just over one month earlier. And, during that phone conversation, she assured me that she could still see only three ripened follicles.

"Maybe there was another follicle hiding behind one of these," she told me. "But there is simply no evidence that there could be more than four. And even if there were four, chances are not all would have been fertilized and not all of those would have implanted in your uterus."

Then she reviewed with me some of the same information I had heard from the nurse in the hospital: that what the technician had seen on the hospital ultrasound might be only the reflections of sacs; that some of the sacs could be empty. She concluded with, "I believe that the hospital ultrasound is not a true picture. You may be carrying twins, or perhaps triplets. I just don't think there can be more than triplets.

"In twenty years of fertility practice, following these procedures, I have never seen a patient who had more than triplets."

We set up an appointment for the following week, Thursday, June 5, so that she could examine me and take more ultrasounds in her office. By that time, she told me, the ultrasound should show whether we had one, two, or three babies.

When I got off the phone, I shared the good news with Kenny's mom. She had come from her home in Mason City, a two-hour drive from Carlisle, to stay with me and help with Mikayla for the week while I recuperated from surgery.

Kenny came home for lunch that day and I told him about my

phone conversation with Dr. Hauser. We both felt much better. We would love to have twins. I'd always kind of wanted twins. If it really was three, Kenny and I agreed, "We can do triplets."

By the following Thursday, Kenny's mother had gone home. He had to work; my mom was at work; and my sister Barbara was taking care of Mikayla. So I had to go to Dr. Hauser's office alone. I was nervous, wondering what they would find and wishing I weren't by myself.

Dr. Hauser examined me, checking to see how my incision was healing. Then she turned me over to the technician for an ultrasound. This one, like the last ultrasound done in the hospital, was the more accurate, internal procedure.

The sonographer moved the wand back and forth, up and down. I watched the monitor as first one baby and then another came into focus. The babies were little more than squiggles on the screen. But they were squiggles with visible heartbeats. This time what we were counting was clearly babies. *These are not just sacs. They're not reflections of sacs. And the sacs are obviously not empty. This is the real thing.*

This technician, unlike the one in the hospital, talked to me while she did the test, explaining each move she made. I watched and listened while she counted back and forth and up and down. From the bottom up and from the top down again. She was not only counting out loud; she was also counting on her fingers. When she went to the fingers of her second hand, I knew we were in trouble.

My worst fears had been confirmed. There really were seven sacs, seven heartbeats, seven babies. *So much for triplets,* I thought.

Dr. Hauser came into the room and the sonographer showed her what we were seeing on the monitor. My heart felt as if it stuttered when Dr. Hauser counted seven babies too.

She had little to say to me that day: I don't think she knew what to say. Dr. Hauser seemed to be flabbergasted.

Even this early, the ultrasound showed that two of the babies were only one-half the size of the other five. So most of what Dr. Hauser talked to me about that day centered around these two babies. Because of their size, she obviously did not think those two would make it.

"What we see today may not be what we will see next week," Dr. Hauser assured me. "Next week, these two may not have beating hearts. Or they may not be there at all."

But that would still leave us with five babies. Quintuplets. How would we handle quints? And what if she was wrong and all seven babies survived? How would we manage seven? It was just too much to think about!

I held on to the thoughts spinning around in my head and kept my composure until I made it to the car. Then I let go and bawled. I drove to Barbara's house to pick up Mikayla—crying all the way there.

I walked in the door and found not only Barbara and Mikayla, but also my mother, who was there in hopes of hearing my news.

"There really are seven," I said, sobbing.

Barbara and Mom hugged me, I hugged them, and I cried. They took turns saying, "Oh, Bobbi, I am so sorry," while I choked out the story of my visit to the doctor. They didn't know what else to say.

They did want to see the ultrasound pictures. We all got excited poring over the Polaroid pictures with me pointing out the different babies.

As Mikayla and I headed for home, all I could think was, *Now, I've got to tell Kenny this news. Again.*

Kenny

When I came home from work that day, I could tell that Bobbi had been crying. I had hardly walked through the door when she told me, "There really are seven. Even Dr. Hauser counted them.

We saw seven hearts beating on the ultrasound. So they are not empty sacs, or reflections of sacs. There really are seven babies."

This time, I didn't get upset. "So it is true," I told Bobbi. "That's okay. If we have seven babies, we'll just have to wait and see how God will provide."

I didn't know what to think. We had been told so many different things and had gone from high to low so many times in the past few weeks that by this point I was a little numb. But I also believe that God was beginning to give me a sense of peace about it.

I knew that we could still lose some or all of the babies. That at the next doctor's visit, they might not find all seven still alive. I knew that if Bobbi lost a baby at this point, her body would just reabsorb the tissue. I even thought, *God can use that natural process to take care of us, to bring down the number of babies. Or He can provide for us if all seven are born. It's up to Him to decide.*

Early in the morning hours of June 7, just two days later, our town had a major storm. Between 2:00 and 3:00 A.M., eighty-mile-an-hour winds ripped through Carlisle. I woke to the sound of the wind gusting and rattling windowpanes. I could hear branches of trees snapping. I got up and paced around the house, looking out the windows and doors. By the glow of the lightning, I could see a large maple tree in our backyard bending in the strong winds. I had Bobbi come and look at it too. We finally decided that, even if it fell, it was not tall enough to reach Mikayla's room at the back of our house. So we left Mikayla asleep in her own bed.

Not much later, we heard the cracking sound of that tree as it split down the middle and crashed to the ground. But we had been right; the branches of the tree did not reach our house. We hated losing it but were relieved that its fall didn't damage our home or our garage.

Later, after Bobbi and I had gone back to bed, we heard another loud crash. This time we felt the vibration. Something had hit the house. I jumped up and looked out the front door. I couldn't see anything in the darkness. So I ran to the back door and looked out. Still nothing. I pulled on a jacket.

"You are *not* going out there now," Bobbi told me. "It's raining cats and dogs. Wait until the storm settles down." So we headed back to bed to sleep restlessly while the storm blew itself out.

The next morning our yard was a mess. The second loud crash we had heard was a large tree in our neighbor's yard coming down in the wind. It had fallen in our direction and the upper branches had brushed the side of our house, near our bedroom. But it hadn't done any real damage.

The storm had created havoc all over town. Trees were blown down, windows broken, a few roofs damaged. The citizens of Carlisle spent that entire Saturday cleaning up broken branches, fallen trees, and other storm debris. Most people were out working in their yards all day. But not everyone: I did not let my pregnant wife help with the cleanup. I didn't want her lifting or hauling anything.

A lot of things might happen, things over which we had no control, that could cause Bobbi to lose one or all of the babies. If so, we would live with that. But I didn't want her to actively do anything that might cause the miscarriage of even one baby. God had somehow given us these babies. They were His to give or take. Our job was to do what we could to protect them.

Bobbi

Kenny had been surprisingly calm when I gave him the news of "seven babies" for the second time. His low-key, accepting response was a welcome relief.

But the day of storm cleanup that first Saturday of June was a taste of unpleasant things to come for me. I stood around and watched friends and neighbors clean up, while I did nothing. And I thought, *This is hard! But it is how it's going to be for a long time. I'm going to have to just sit and watch the world go by.*

The next week was Kenny's vacation. We had planned all along, when he signed up for this time off, for this to be a stay-at-home, working vacation. We wanted to remodel our bathroom, and we planned to have some relaxing family time with Mikayla.

Our trip to the Blank Park Zoo in Des Moines turned out to be a fun family event. Kenny and I laughed at Mikayla, who was more interested in the rocks along the paths than she was in the animals in the cages.

Most of all Mikayla liked the big yellow and white carplike fish in a large pond in an open area of the zoo. I watched while Kenny and Mikayla went around and around the plank walkway that circled the pond. As they walked, Kenny let Mikayla get closer and closer to the fish she seemed so fascinated with, until I was terrified that she would jump in and try to grab one of them.

That was a memorable day. We had no idea it would be our last family outing for a long time.

Most of that week, Kenny, Mikayla, and I spent together out in our yard or working on our bathroom. We removed and replaced our old vanity and Kenny installed a new faucet. We also hung a new wallpaper border. And since Kenny was off work, he was able to go with me at the end of that week when I made another visit to Dr. Hauser.

We started that appointment out with another ultrasound. I have to admit I was hoping for less than seven to show up this time. But all seven were there. And as far as they could tell, all seven were bigger and seemed healthy. The doctor could no longer tell any significant difference in the babies' sizes. The two babies who had been smaller on the ultrasound last week had caught up in size.

The babies were no longer just squiggles with heartbeats. I was seven and a half weeks along now. We could see the babies' heads and the general shape of their bodies. And, of course, we could see their hearts beating.

Kenny

I was glad to finally be able to go with Bobbi to the doctor. I'd never before seen a live ultrasound. With all the ultrasounds Bobbi had with Mikayla, I had not been able to get off work to go with her. So I'd had to content myself with the Polaroids. This was all new stuff for me.

We took Mikayla along with us, to be together as a family, just as we had always taken Mikayla with us wherever we could.

While Bobbi lay on the table and the sonographer conducted the test, Mikayla sat on my lap. We all watched the screen. First one baby came into focus. We could see his little head and there, on the screen, his little heart was beating. Then the technician moved the probe and another baby came up on the monitor. Another head, with another beating heart. *These are babies!* I thought. *And there are seven of them. Amazing!*

Bobbi

After the ultrasound was finished, Dr. Hauser talked to us in her office. She told us that it was time for us to move on to another doctor. A fertility specialist only carries her patients past the point of getting pregnant. Then most women transfer their care to an obstetrician. Dr. Hauser told us that, rather than seeing a regular OB, as we had done with Mikayla, she would recommend we go to a perinatologist. When I asked her what that meant, she told us that a perinatologist is an obstetrician for high-risk pregnancies.

She recommended a practice with two perinatologists at Iowa Methodist Medical Center in Des Moines, or another doctor in Cedar Rapids. Neither Kenny nor I wanted to commute the two hours to Cedar Rapids for every appointment. So, Dr. Hauser told us she would call Drs. Drake and Mahone at Iowa Methodist and set up an appointment for us.

As we drove home that afternoon, my emotions were still going crazy. Seeing the babies' hearts beating was exhilarating. Seeing Kenny's excited reaction to the ultrasound was heart-warming. But I still didn't want seven babies.

That night I wrote in my journal:

I just wish I could understand what God is trying to teach us.
I know to trust Him, but what else? There must be more.

Our last visit with Dr. Hauser had been on Friday, June 13. The following Monday, June 16, Dr. Paula Mahone, the perinatologist, called. She told me that she liked to talk to her patients personally; she wanted to let us know what would take place during the first appointment.

"This will not be a 'We're so happy you are pregnant' type of visit," she told me. "You will have a physical examination and perhaps an ultrasound. Then we will have a consultation. There are numerous risks associated with multiple births. We'll have a lot of information for you to sort through." She asked me to bring anyone who would be involved in the pregnancy with us to the appointment, so they would also be aware of what to expect.

Then she told me that we could discuss what options we might exercise if we decided we didn't want all the babies.

I knew that she was referring to "selective reduction," a procedure in which drugs are injected into a baby's heart to make it stop beating. Selective reduction causes that selected baby to abort, usually without risking other babies in the pregnancy.

"I am a Christian," I told her. "I am not willing to consider selective reduction. I believe that life starts at conception. Selective reduction is abortion, and abortion is killing a human life. I believe that is wrong. That is not something I am interested in. And I am not going to go to a doctor who is going to pressure me every week to do something I think is wrong."

"I am a Christian too," she answered. "If that is the way you feel, no one in this office will bring up the subject again. That is a closed subject . . . unless something changes and your life is in jeopardy. If we end up with seven babies and no mother, we will not view that as a success. Your life must come first."

That phone call lasted more than thirty minutes. I hung up thinking that I liked Dr. Mahone, that she sounded nice. And she was true to her word: No one in her office suggested selective reduction to us again.

The decision against the use of selective reduction was an easy one for us. We both knew how we felt about abortion of any kind: Abortion is the taking of a life. We knew we wanted to choose life. But we had no way of knowing that this was just the first of many life-and-death decisions we would be asked to make.

Six

We Can't Do This!

Bobbi

*T*here are many potential complications with multiple births," Dr. Mahone said. "They include diabetes, anemia, toxemia, blood disorders, spontaneous abortions, and premature labor."

It was June 23, our first appointment with the perinatologists. Just as Dr. Mahone had suggested, Kenny and I took my sister Barbara, his stepmother, Val, and my mother along for the trip. Unfortunately, the office was way behind schedule when we arrived for our appointment. Someone eventually came out and apologized for the delay, explaining that they had admitted four patients to the hospital already that day. But the delay meant that my mother had to leave for work before we were able to see the doctor.

When we finally started with the consultation, Dr. Mahone went through everything I ever could have thought about concerning multiple, high-risk births. After discussing all the possible complications, she went on to talk about the probability of exten-sive bed rest and the certainty of hospitalization by the twentieth week of pregnancy. She told me, "No more lifting or housework. We want you to rest as much as possible." By the time she finished, the doctor had been so thorough that none of us could think of any questions she had not already answered.

I headed to another room for a physical examination. Dr. Mahone started with a breast exam, then an abdominal exam. Both went fine. But when she checked my cervix, we ran into problems.

My cervix was not dilated at all, yet the doctor could fit two fingers into the opening. "It should be closed tightly," she said, explaining that she now felt it was imperative to immediately do an ultrasound to check the length of my cervix.

That ultrasound showed the length of the cervix was fine. So I wasn't dilated and had not begun to efface. "But it shouldn't have been open at all," Dr. Mahone said again.

Kenny

The consultation was so full of information, it was enough to make my head spin. Then the physical exam didn't go well. Something was wrong with Bobbi's cervix.

My heart sank when Dr. Mahone told Bobbi: "This means you are on complete bed rest, starting now. We need to keep the weight of the babies off your cervix as much as possible."

Then she explained, in detail, just what complete bed rest would mean. "Bobbi may be up no more than two to three hours a day—just enough for showers, going to the bathroom, and meals. Absolutely no housework and no lifting at all, not even Mikayla. And no driving: From now on someone will have to drive you to and from your appointments. Do not go anywhere else. And we will have to see you every week, not just every other week."

We had known that Bobbi would eventually have to go on bed rest. But we certainly hadn't thought that she would have to be off her feet so soon! When I thought of all the extra work that would mean for me . . . it was overwhelming, to say the least.

"I know this won't be easy," the doctor told us. "But it may make the difference between life and death for your babies."

Then we went in for another ultrasound to check on the babies. Nine weeks along now, the babies had arms and legs and looked like real babies. We could see them kick and move around. We could see their hearts beating. We got to see parts of all seven babies. That was thrilling! Somehow that really clinched it for me; seeing the babies like that. These really were babies and all seven of them were *ours*.

Bobbi

At the final visit with Dr. Hauser, just ten days earlier, I had been hoping to see less than seven heartbeats on the ultrasound monitor, still wishing this pregnancy was a little more in line with what we had planned. But somehow, by this visit, I found myself looking at the screen, hoping that we would find seven beating hearts and a little concerned that one of the babies would be missing. I was surprised to realize that I was relieved to see them all there on the monitor, kicking and moving around.

We saw good pictures of all seven babies. That hadn't happened before. *And, it probably won't happen again*, I thought. *After this they'll be getting too big for a picture this good.*

Kenny

On the way home, my feelings roller-coastered up and down. When I remembered seeing the babies on the ultrasound, I got excited again. The sight of seven wiggling babies and seven hearts beating had been absolutely amazing!

However, when I thought about the new demands on my time, I got worried. Now I was going to have to come home from work and do all the laundry and housework and all the caring for Mikayla.

The doctor had told Bobbi that she would have to quit work. Bobbi was still working part-time as a seamstress for the Bridal Connection, altering bridal gowns at home. We had been counting on Bobbi's income to pay for our health insurance. All I could think was: *What will we do without that income? How can we pay for our health insurance premiums, plus pay back the cost of fertility treatments? We can't afford all this. How are we going to do it?*

Bobbi

July 4, a week and a half later, was a big, feel-sorry-for-myself day. I was already tired of my daily bed rest routine. I would sleep as late in the morning as eighteen-month-old Mikayla would let me. Then I would shower and dress and move from my bed to the couch in the living room. Sometimes, for a change, I'd lie on a lounge chair.

Kenny's stepmother, Val, came over every weekday to help with Mikayla. She would stay through the morning and get Mikayla's lunch for me. We would put Mikayla down for a nap at 2:00 P.M., and I took a nap too. Val would go home for a while, but came back at 3:30 P.M. and waited for Mikayla to wake up. She took Mikayla to her house for the rest of the day so that I could continue to nap. I tried to sleep each day from two to six in the afternoon.

Kenny would pick up Mikayla when he got off work. Then I would be up for a while after Kenny and Mikayla got home in the evening. Even with all that sleep, I still felt tired all the time.

By July 4, 1997, I was ready to cheat a little on my bed rest. We drove to Market Street to see the parade. I lay on the lounge chair to watch a typical Carlisle, Iowa, holiday parade: The town's fire engine started it off and was followed by about 101 T-ball, softball, and baseball teams marching down the street, carrying banners. During the parade, both Kenny and I were freezing cold. So we went back home and changed into warmer clothes before we drove over to Kenny's dad's house for a family Fourth of July celebration.

Dad and Val's backyard joins North Park, the big community park in Carlisle. From their deck, we could see the booths of the Fourth of July carnival in the park. Lying on my lounge chair, I could see friends and neighbors buying funnel cakes and playing games. I could hear the splashing sounds of the mayor and other local politicians getting dunked in the dunking booth.

After a while, Kenny and I walked across to the gazebo in the park, where I lay down on my lounge chair again. We listened to Kenny's brother Matt play in the high school jazz band, and later, with the community band.

When we went back to Dad and Val's house, I lay on the lounge chair and watched while Kenny and his brothers grilled burgers and had a good time.

The worst moment of the whole miserable day came when Mikayla hurt herself. She was playing with a plastic straw in her mouth and crawled up the step to the patio where I was lying down. She bumped the straw on the step, and it made a small cut on the roof of her mouth.

I called her over to me and, after a moment or two, she came. I could see that her mouth was bleeding. Val came out of the house, picked up Mikayla, and offered to take her over to the park and buy her some ice cream. I knew that the cold of the ice cream would help the bleeding stop. And I was glad that Val could take her.

But I wanted to cry. All I could think was: *She is my child and I can't even help her when she is hurt. I couldn't go to her and I couldn't pick her up. I just had to sit here on this chair by myself and do nothing. I can't help with the burgers or even mix the salad. All I can do is watch and listen while others have a good time.*

That night we watched the fireworks from the deck of Dad and Val's house. When we went home a little later I couldn't help thinking, *This day hasn't been fun at all.*

After that night I thought about my obligations. I felt an obligation to these babies. I needed to do whatever I could to ensure their safety. But I also had a prior commitment to my daughter, Mikayla, who still needed a mother. And I had a responsibility to Kenny, who still needed a wife. I decided that it would be okay for me to "cheat" a little on my bed rest, in order to maintain some sanity and to balance my obligations as wife and mother.

Kenny

On July 4, Bobbi had "cheated" on her bed rest, going to the parade and over to Dad and Val's house. And on another occasion she went with Mikayla and me to an evening church service. There she reclined on a lounge chair in the aisle of the sanctuary. No damage was done.

So, when she decided to go to church again the following Friday evening, we didn't think very much about it. We had no idea it would cause us our first really big scare.

That had been the week of Vacation Bible School at our church. Bobbi's eleven-year-old brother, Dennis, had a role in the Friday evening closing program. We hauled Bobbi's lounge chair over to the church and set it up in the aisle, so Bobbi could see Dennis perform.

And, during the program, everything did seem to be okay.

Bobbi

It felt good to be out among people, seeing friends and family at church that Friday night. I enjoyed the VBS program. And as long as I was lying on the lounge chair, I felt fine. It was after the program, when I tried to stand up, that I felt something in my abdomen give . . . or pull.

I didn't think a lot about it at first. My brother Pete came over to where I was standing, and he and I talked. Then I felt some wetness. Startled, and suddenly afraid, I pulled my dress around, right there in the aisle of the church. What I saw looked like spots of blood.

I ran to the bathroom to check and I was definitely bleeding and leaking a clear fluid. I immediately walked from the bathroom and grabbed Kenny.

"We've got to go to the hospital," I told him.

"Why?" he asked.

"I'm bleeding . . . and I think I'm leaking fluid."

"Oh, no!"

My mother overheard what we were saying. "I'll go with you!" she said. My brother Pete and his wife, Linda, were there and offered to keep Mikayla.

Kenny, my mom, and I ran for the car. The word must have spread quickly in the congregation: By the time I was lying in the backseat of the car and Kenny was climbing into the driver's seat, Pastor Brown came running out.

"Let's pray before you go," he suggested. And standing there beside the open door of our car, Pastor prayed for Kenny and me and for our babies. The moment he finished, we took off for Iowa Methodist Medical Center in Des Moines.

Kenny

I drove as fast as I thought it was safe to go. But it wasn't fast enough for my anxious mother-in-law. When I stopped at the first red light we came to on Army Post Road, Peggy told me, "Run it! Run the red light!" But that seemed too dangerous to me, so I stopped. The same scene repeated itself at every red light we encountered on the way to Iowa Methodist Medical Center in downtown Des Moines.

Peggy also wanted me to drive faster, saying, "If the police try to stop you for speeding, just keep going. They can be a police escort! We can explain when we get to the hospital." But no police came along in the half hour it took us to get to the emergency room.

We must be losing the babies, I thought. I was scared to death. Bobbi and I had both reached the point where we really wanted these babies. *Which baby isn't going to be there when we get to the hospital?* I wondered. *What is happening? Lord, what are You doing? Lord, please protect Bobbi. And please protect our babies.*

Bobbi

When we arrived at the emergency room door, my mother jumped out of the car and ran into the hospital.

"Quick," she told the people at the desk right inside the door. "My daughter is pregnant with seven babies and she is bleeding. You've got to get a stretcher and come get her."

The hospital personnel looked at her as if she were crazy. "We don't have any stretchers," they told her. "She'll just have to walk in. Then we'll get her in a wheelchair."

"She can't walk in!" my mother protested. "She could be losing one of the babies!"

"Well, if she really needs a stretcher, you can take her around to the ambulance entrance."

When Mom raced back outside to tell us that, I decided the bleeding seemed to have slowed down and I could just walk in. Once I had found a wheelchair in the ER, Kenny began to fill out the paperwork for my admission. And I had begun to really bleed again. Mom and I waited for a while before a triage doctor came out and began asking me questions.

"What seems to be the problem?" he asked.

"I am pregnant with seven babies," I told him. "I am bleeding and passing fluid. I'm afraid I'm losing one of the babies!"

"How far along are you?" he asked.

"Twelve weeks," I answered.

"And when did this start?" he asked.

I thought we would take forever to cover my history. And so did my mother. At one point, she announced to everyone within earshot, "This is certainly nothing like *ER* on TV. Nobody in this place hurries!"

"Mother!" I exclaimed, embarrassed.

"Well, it's true!" she answered. If the emergency room personnel heard her, they didn't seem to be offended. But then they didn't speed up at all, either.

I was finally taken back to an examination room. Kenny was still in Admitting. My mother had to stay in the waiting area.

A nurse came back with me and began to ask me many of the same questions that the triage doctor had asked.

"Now, what seems to be wrong?" she asked.

"I am pregnant with more than one baby," I began.

"How many?" she asked.

"Seven."

The nurse looked at me for a long moment before continuing.

"Why do you think there is a problem?"

"I am losing fluid and blood," I told her. While answering her questions I had been sitting on the examination table. When I got up to put on a hospital gown, I left a big wet spot on the table.

"Oh, I think you are right!" the nurse exclaimed. As I put on the gown, she left and shortly came back with a second nurse.

"Can my husband come back here with me?" I asked them.

"Oh, the doctor on duty doesn't like to have the family in the exam rooms," the second nurse told me.

"Who cares?" responded the first nurse. "Just go get her husband!"

After she went, the first nurse left to go get me a blanket because I was feeling cold. When she came back she reassured me, "Don't worry about that doctor. We already contacted Dr. Drake. She's on her way in and she's having you transferred up to

Labor and Delivery. They have ultrasounds and everything they'll need to examine you there."

An aide wheeled me upstairs to the obstetrics ward on a gurney as Kenny walked alongside me, holding my hand. Once we got there, an OB nurse came to take my history, again. She asked, "Is it really true? That you are going to have seven babies?"

"Yes," I told her.

She paused for a moment. "Did you *want* seven babies?"

"Well, it's not what I ordered," I told her. And I thought: *What kind of person would just decide "Yeah, let's have seven babies"?*

"Well, I didn't think so," the nurse said. "But I wanted to make sure."

I have since thought of many things I might have said in response: "Yeah, we just didn't think quads or quints would be enough of a challenge." Or, "Actually we were going for a full baseball team; we just came up a couple short." Or, "Our daughter loves the story of Snow White so much we thought we'd give her seven siblings to play the part of her 'dwarfs.'" But I didn't think of any of those at the time.

A few moments later, when she left the room and closed the door behind her, I looked at Kenny and rolled my eyes. He grinned and shook his head in disbelief. *As if anyone would deliberately choose to have seven babies at one time. Forget Labor and Delivery—take me right to the psych ward.*

Finally Dr. Karen Drake, Dr. Mahone's partner, arrived and began the first examination I'd had since arriving at the hospital. I had been nervous and scared; just seeing Dr. Drake's familiar smiling face helped me feel better. But that didn't last long.

"Your cervix is the same as it has been, Bobbi. But it looks like you are bleeding from inside the uterus." Dr. Drake's announcement was not good news. "Let's see what an ultrasound tells us."

An ultrasound machine was wheeled in and Dr. Drake began to check out the babies. I watched the monitor, wondering how many babies we had left.

Much to our surprise, seven babies and seven heartbeats were still there. And all seven babies had the correct amount of amniotic fluid.

"I just don't see where the fluid, or the blood, is coming from," Dr. Drake concluded. "But it looks like everything is okay now."

Kenny

All the way to the hospital, all the time I had been doing the paperwork to have Bobbi admitted, I had assumed that we were losing babies. I was also worried for Bobbi. I kept asking myself, *Who isn't going to be there when they do an ultrasound?*

To have everything still be okay was amazing to me. *Wow,* I thought. *Somebody should be missing. And they are not! Every one of our babies is still fine and dandy. Thank You, Lord.*

Seven

Doubt

Bobbi

The babies look fine. As long as the amount of bleeding doesn't increase I don't think we need to be overly concerned," Dr. Drake concluded. "A little bleeding at this stage of pregnancy isn't at all uncommon. A lot of times we never know the reason."

What a relief! I really had been scared I was losing one of the babies.

"What were you doing when the bleeding started? Where were you?" the doctor asked.

I had no choice but to tell the truth. "At church," I admitted very softly, unable to lie about that and hoping she would not quite understand my words. Or simply let it pass. No such luck.

"What?" Dr. Drake exclaimed. "Did you say 'church'? What in the world were you doing at church? Didn't we tell you you were on bed rest?"

I made a feeble attempt at self-defense. "I was in a lounge chair," I told her.

"I don't care what you were sitting in," the doctor replied. "It's not just hard pews we're worried about; there's the car ride, unnecessary bumps and jolts. From now on, no more church! Do you understand?" I nodded a meek and silent response. "From now on the church will have to come to you. I think the Lord will understand!

"And one more thing: Next time anything unusual happens, call first. If we can talk over the phone first we may be able to save both you and me an unnecessary trip to the hospital."

"Okay," I agreed. I'd never once thought about calling. I'd just panicked.

Driving home from the hospital late that night I felt chastised, but grateful. *Thank You, Lord, that all the babies are okay.* In the brief course of that thought, that silent sentence prayer, I realized just how far my feelings had progressed these past few weeks. From desperately praying that "seven sacs" had been a mistake, to half hoping the weekly ultrasounds would show only five, or even four remaining babies, to the genuine gratitude I felt that all the babies were still there.

I was only twelve weeks along. Everything I read and everything the medical experts told me said it was impossible. There was no way I could deliver septuplets. In my head, I knew that. But my heart could no longer accept that verdict; it was already sailing a different course. Every instinct in my being, every emotion I felt as a mother, testified to my soul that those weren't just blips on the ultrasound screen. Those "images" were obviously babies. *Our* babies.

I understood the odds against them. All the medical personnel involved were still assuming that I would lose some or all of the babies. But despite the emotional risk, despite the cost, I loved them already. And I realized I now wanted every one.

But that didn't mean I had to like my doctors' orders. I certainly didn't. On the one hand I was convinced I would go crazy if I had to stay in bed for the next five or six months!

On the other hand, a part of me determined to do whatever it took, because I so desperately wanted those babies.

Kenny

I hadn't reached the point Bobbi had. I was still struggling to accept the very idea of a large multiple birth; I simply wasn't yet able to embrace the reality of seven babies.

Seeing all those images on the ultrasound had thrilled me. Anyone could see the heads, the bodies, the little arms and legs. They were obviously babies. And that meant there were clearly seven of them in Bobbi's uterus. That much I understood.

I think I also realized that Bobbi had already formed an emotional bond with those babies—all seven of them. The incredible and mysterious emotional and spiritual bond pregnant women experience and we "pregnant fathers" can appreciate and marvel at, but never fully comprehend.

On some level I probably worried about the reaction Bobbi was going to have if, or more likely *when,* we lost some or all of the babies as everyone assumed would happen. But it wasn't so much the fear of emotional involvement and its risk of pain that prevented me from accepting the idea of seven babies. I think my problem was an inability to face, let alone deal with, the overwhelming future implications of that possibility.

I was feeling overwhelmed enough by the immediate demands of this pregnancy. I'm the kind of person who needs a predictable routine. I value consistency over variety. I appreciate stability far more than I like surprises. I hate having my carefully laid plans disrupted. I've got a controlling type personality. And while I'm not what most people would consider an introspective person, I know these things about myself.

That is why from time to time in those first weeks and months of the pregnancy I would find myself questioning God. *If I know the kind of person I am, You certainly should, Lord. You created me. So what in the world can You be thinking? Seven babies? I'm just not ready for this. And I don't think I ever will be.*

Bobbi has always been the take-charge person on the home front. And, like a lot of husbands, I'd often taken my wife for granted. But the more the summer of 1997 progressed and the more of Bobbi's household duties I took over, the more I appreciated the sacrifices Bobbi had always made for our family.

It wasn't as if I had to take up all the slack by myself. Both our families were wonderfully supportive. My stepmother, Val, a kindergarten teacher at nearby Carlisle Elementary, volunteered to care for Mikayla until she had to go back to school in August. The few days Val had conflicting plans, Bobbi's sister Michele, a twenty-year-old college student, would come over to be with our active toddler.

Family weren't the only ones who demonstrated true generosity. Neighbors were quick to offer any kind of assistance we needed. And the thoughtful response of our church was almost overwhelming. No sooner had our doctors put Bobbi on bed rest than our Missionary Baptist friends passed out a sign-up sheet for volunteers who began delivering home-cooked meals three days a week at suppertime.

Still, even with all the extra help, there seemed to be more than ever for me to do when I got home from work each night. I'd never realized how much laundry and housework Bobbi had done over the years.

On the plus side, the increase in my parenting responsibilities drew me closer to my daughter. The two of us went out for breakfast every Saturday morning so Bobbi could sleep in. And whenever I had chores to do or errands to run, I took Mikayla with me. I took her grocery shopping, to the post office, and we even managed to take in a few church softball league games. All that one-on-one time strengthened the bonds between us and raised our father-daughter relationship to a whole new level. It was wonderful.

But there was also a very sobering downside. The more time I spent with my one-and-a-half-year-old daughter and the greater responsibility I assumed for her care, the harder it was not to let my imagination multiply everything by seven and begin to feel overwhelmed about the future.

It was one thing, when I was alone in my own daily quiet time, to remember and review the biblical promises of God that Pastor Brown had shared with me when I'd been shell-shocked the day we were first told Bobbi was pregnant with seven babies. I could assure myself that it was all true:

God wasn't going to give us more than we could handle. At least not without giving us the resources we needed (1 Corinthians 10:13).

God really could supply all our needs according to His riches in glory (Philippians 4:19).

As the apostle Paul said, "I can do all things through Christ who strengthens me" (Philippians 4:13).

Those seemed such encouraging promises when Pastor shared them with me and when I reread them in my Bible. I did have days when I was able to keep those promises in focus and feel upbeat about life.

But I had many more days when they were all too easy to forget— when I felt overwhelmed, even a little frustrated, by my newly added responsibilities of parenting one child and began to imagine the challenges multiplied by seven.

Whenever Mikayla awakened crying in the night, I'd rock her back to sleep, wondering: *How are we ever going to get any sleep with seven?* Sitting at the breakfast table, trying in vain to coax an eighteen-month-old to eat enough to sustain her through the morning before I left for work could get frustrating. *What kind of ordeal would mealtime be with seven fussy babies?*

I vividly remember one Sunday morning when I'd finally won the battle with a squirming Mikayla to get her dress and then her socks on. We were already running late for church when we got to her shoes. Or rather shoe. I got the first one on only to realize I'd dropped or misplaced the second. By the time I found it, Daddy's precious little girl had pulled off the other one and both socks.

That was when I just lost it. I gave up and began pacing around the house ranting and raving: "I don't believe this! I can't get one child dressed and to church on time. What are we gonna do when we have eight kids to get dressed? It'll be impossible! I can't do this! We'll never get anywhere on time again!" And on and on I went.

By the time I finally calmed down I think Bobbi had Mikayla's shoes and socks back on. And my daughter and I headed off to church, a bit later and more in need of peace, inspiration, and encouragement than usual for a Sunday morning.

But what got to me more than daily demands and the routine frustrations of parenting were the impending financial questions.

I've always been cautious and conservative when it comes to money. Bobbi would probably say I tend to get uptight about money issues. And she'd be right. But I'd had to be—even with only one child.

How are we ever going to afford eight?

I still hadn't figured out where we were going to find enough money in our monthly budget just to pay our health insurance premiums, which Bobbi's part-time income had covered before. I knew enough about multiple births to know that there could be astronomical expenses even our good insurance plan wouldn't cover. And what about the routine day-to-day expenses required to feed and clothe a large family?

We were soon going to need more than our five-passenger Oldsmobile. But there was no way we could afford to be thinking about buying a new car on top of everything else. *Maybe I can trade for an old van I can fix up?*

But where and how were we going to live? *With just under 800 square feet, we're already cramped with three of us. There is not enough room for ten of us. We could move, but where? We can't afford the mortgage payments on a bigger house. We'll have to add on. But that, too, will mean borrowing money, bigger monthly payments, and more taxes.*

There seemed no way around it. We were going to need more money. There was no realistic way Bobbi could get a job. She was going to have her hands full at home. There aren't that many jobs in Carlisle, Iowa. If we moved somewhere else I might have been able to earn more, but we would lose the support network of family, friends, and church.

I kept worrying and telling myself, *You're gonna have to do something.* I started thinking about getting a second job. The trouble with that plan was that, as long as Bobbi was on bed rest, I already had a second job at home as Mr. Mom. *No way can I be gone from home any more hours of the day!* But, *What if I could figure out a way to earn extra money at home?* I'd done a little detailing of cars in the past. I'd enjoyed it and was good at it. *That's it! I can start my own detailing business. It's something I can do evenings and weekends—on my own time.*

Two problems quickly made me realize the impracticality of that idea. The doctors said Bobbi was going to be bedridden for the remainder of this pregnancy, which meant that I was going to have no time of my own for months. And I knew I was fooling myself to think I was going to have any more time once the babies were born. If Mikayla was taking as much of my time and energy as she did, what would we do with seven more? Even if we ended up with five, or four, or just three, I now realized our babies were going to take all the time and energy Bobbi and I could possibly give. And then some.

And the sobering truth was, even if I somehow managed to carve out the time to do a little detailing, the extra few hundred dollars a month I could hope for (at best), couldn't begin to put a dent in the staggering expenses I could see looming larger and larger in the too-near future.

The more I thought about it, the bigger our financial dilemma looked, the more impossible our situation seemed, and the more helpless I felt. The more time I spent desperately trying to dream up a solution, the more new expenses I began to anticipate and the more discouraged I got.

Looking back I can see how easy it would have been for me to have a serious nervous breakdown.

Maybe if the challenge hadn't seemed so hopelessly insurmountable that might have happened. As it was, I think the sheer impossibility of the problem we faced may have saved me from complete emotional meltdown. I quickly came to the conclusion that our financial situation was so hopeless I could do absolutely nothing that would make a significant difference. I had no choice but to throw up my hands and say, "I give up. There's nothing humanly possible to be done. This is just not a Kenny-size problem. This is a God-size problem. There is absolutely no sense in my worrying anymore. It's all gotta be up to You, Lord!"

There was a very real sense of relief when I got to that stage. I realized even then that I'd learned an important lesson. *This isn't just my problem anymore. It's God's problem as well. No matter what happens, He's going to help.*

I believed that. I really did. But that didn't mean I wasn't going to sometimes forget that truth in the difficult days and weeks to come.

Bobbi

While Kenny's emotional ups and downs focused mostly on imagined future financial concerns, I was far more discouraged by the very real constraints of my frustrating here and now.

For the first five months of the pregnancy, I was plagued with morning-noon-and-night sickness. Only once was I sick enough to actually throw up; the rest of the time I just felt nauseous.

Feeling sick all the time didn't help me eat. And I needed to eat. The doctors kept encouraging me to gain more weight. That was hard to do when I didn't feel like eating. I certainly never wanted to eat the 4,000-calorie-a-day diet my doctors recommended.

Being confined to bed was maddening. Kenny got Mikayla up every morning and fed her breakfast before Val arrived and he left for work. I slept as late as I could because there was really nothing to wake up for. The earlier I awakened, the more hours I'd have to do nothing but feel frustrated.

I did read a lot of books on those long summer days. But even as much as I loved to read and had always longed for more time to do so, I soon got my fill. There was a boring sameness to my daily routine that even a good novel couldn't dispel.

I appreciated everything everyone was doing for me. I just hated the fact that they had to be doing it and I couldn't.

I especially appreciated the way Kenny pitched in and took over with Mikayla. On the one hand I enjoyed seeing their relationship blossom and grow as he spent more and more time feeding, dressing, changing, and bathing our little girl. On the other hand I envied, and sometimes perhaps resented, the experiences he shared with her.

I particularly remember the sense of frustration I felt when Wal-Mart had their big annual closeout sale on kids' summer clothes (which they have about the middle of the summer). It was a wonderful chance to purchase what Mikayla would need the following year, to get some great buys, and a time for me as a mother to dream about my little girl being another year older. But I had to abdicate the whole enjoyable experience to Kenny for whom it was a major chore. And I hated that.

I was so bored and discouraged by my predicament that I didn't much feel like celebrating my birthday when July 18 rolled around. Family came over to share cake and ice cream, and there were presents, of course. But after the VBS scare the previous week, Kenny wasn't about to take me anywhere. So it seemed too much like any other boring summer day. The only significant difference being that I was now twenty-nine years old and I didn't want to be. It wasn't what I would call a "happy" birthday at all.

The long, hot summer dragged on and on. The biggest highlight, the only thing I found worth writing about in my journal most weeks, was my weekly checkup. On July 21, I wrote:

> Just another routine visit with the doctor. My cervix hasn't changed at all, the babies are growing, and my weight is good. They found the reason for the bleeding. One of the placentas bled underneath its membrane and formed a clot. The clot liquefied and bled off. It's nothing to be worried about. I guess it's a common occurrence.

A week later, on July 28, I wrote:

> I'm fourteen weeks now, but I look and measure at least twice that big. I'm not too uncomfortable yet, though. I went to the doctor again today. It seems like a lot of visits, but I like it. This way, I get to see the babies every week. That makes me feel better. The ultrasound tech was new this week . . . so it took a long time to complete it. Everything still looks wonderful.

The next doctor's visit was not exactly boring, or wonderful. The babies had already settled into position in my uterus. Baby A was on the bottom, nearest my cervix. He would be nicknamed "Hercules," because he seemed to be holding the others up in an inverse pyramid. Above Baby A, Babies B and C were side by side. Just above them was Baby D. And Babies E, F, and G were in an arc at the top. Although they kicked and squirmed around in their own little corners, they no longer had room to change their positions in my uterus.

Dr. Drake was doing the ultrasound that day. Lying on the exam table, I could see the ultrasound picture on the television in the corner of the room. As usual she started at the bottom, checking for seven heartbeats. First, there on the screen I could see Baby A's heart pulsing. Then she moved the wand up toward Babies B and C. But she found only one heartbeat there. Maybe the babies had shifted a little. She counted on up, finding heartbeats for Babies D, E, F, and G. Then she started at the bottom again, counting slower this time. She still found only six heartbeats.

Oh, no! I thought. *We've lost one. What everyone has been telling us would happen, has happened. We have lost a baby.* I tried to tell myself, *You still have six babies, Bobbi.* My eyes started to burn with tears, just thinking, *But we have lost one of our babies!*

Finally, after twenty minutes of poring over the ultrasound, Dr. Drake went back, one more time, very, very slowly. And there was the seventh heartbeat, pulsing on the screen. Baby B and Baby C had been so close to each other, head to head, that we had been seeing only one heartbeat, where there had been two.

I held my tears in the doctor's office. I didn't even cry on the way home with Val. But, once home, I called my mother and told her about the missing heartbeat. That's when I broke down and cried.

My journal entry for August 5 adds this:

Today at the doctor I found I must suffer yet another "humiliation." From now on, between the car and the doctor's office, I have to ride in a wheelchair. Since I'm progressing they want me off my feet as much as possible.

Next week we start doing anatomy scans on the babies—a couple at a time. This is to check for any possible birth defects. Some potential problems they wouldn't be able to see until later. But this is a good start.

Doubt

My summer had gone back to its boring routine. I didn't make another entry until after the next weekly appointment on August 12 when I wrote:

This is a week of changes. Val had to go back to work, so she won't be staying here to help with Mikayla during the day anymore. Michele plans to be here in a couple of days to take up where Val left off. And Mom will start taking me to my doctor visits. That started today.

We also started looking closely at the anatomy of the babies. It's quite a lengthy process. We only checked out three this first time. All three look wonderful. Dr. Drake used the word *phenomenal*. They were all just as big as they should be. All the internal organs were present. The brains were divided into two halves and the hearts look good too. Everything was just perfect!

We also got to tell what the sexes were. Baby A is a boy. Babies B and C are girls. We'll find out about the next two in another week.

What we didn't know at that point was that before another week of my routine, boring summer was over, we were going to experience a lot more excitement than I really wanted.

Eight

Seventeen-Week Crisis

Bobbi

On Sunday morning, August 18, I was all alone at home, in my bedroom, confined to bed, and feeling very sorry for myself again. Kenny and Mikayla had left for church almost two hours earlier. I could picture them sitting without me near the front of the sanctuary with at least two pews full of my family.

This was a big day of celebration for the Hepworth clan. My brother Pete and his wife, Linda, were dedicating their baby daughter, Melissa, who had been born two weeks after our Memorial Day camping trip. My parents and all my siblings were at Missionary Baptist Church that hot August morning for the big family event. And I was home in bed—again.

Melissa was Pete and Linda's first child, so I had extra reason for wanting to be there. Extra reason to feel left out.

The family all planned on coming to our house for a big cookout after the service. At least I wouldn't have to miss out on that.

In fact, I thought, checking the clock on the nightstand, *Pete should have been here by now.* The dedication had been scheduled near the start of the service. Pete had planned to slip out after the ceremony and hurry over to our house to get the charcoal fired up and the ground beef made into hamburger patties. *It's after 11:30. Something must have happened.*

I knew Kenny would be upset with me if I went outside and fussed over the grill. *But if someone doesn't get started on the preparation soon, we won't be able to eat until mid-afternoon. And everybody is going to be starved. I can at least work on the burgers.*

I went out to the kitchen, took the meat out of the refrigerator, and sat down at the kitchen table to begin shaping patties. No sooner did I have the first layer of a platter filled than I felt a sharp pain shooting through my right side. I felt it a second time just a minute or two later. *Something is wrong! Maybe I strained a muscle pressing out the hamburger patties.* I didn't really believe that. But I didn't want to think it was anything serious.

It was a little after noon when I heard the front door open and Mom and Barbara came in. I had just finished the hamburger patties.

"What are you doing up?" Mom asked when she saw me sitting at the table.

"I just got up to start the burgers," I told her. "I haven't been up long."

"They had the dedication at the end of the service instead of the beginning," Mom explained. "Pete couldn't get away early. Let's see what Barbara and I can do to help."

My mother and sister walked into the kitchen to begin meal preparations, and I got up and headed for my bedroom. When I lay down, I realized that Barbara had followed me. She knew me well enough to realize something wasn't right.

"Are you okay, Bobbi?" Barbara wanted to know.

"I don't know," I replied. "I've been having a real sharp, stabbing pain in my side."

"You're not having contractions are you?" my sister asked. She'd been with me at the first visit with the perinatologists to hear the list of possible complications with a multiple pregnancy—one of the most serious and common of which was premature labor.

"I'm not sure," I told her. "It doesn't feel like any contraction I ever had with Mikayla. I just know it hurts!"

Barbara called my mom in and after hearing what I had to say, Mom hurried out to find Kenny, who was out in the backyard setting up the grill. He rushed in a minute or two later.

"What's wrong?" he asked.

I described the pain.

"Do we need to go to the hospital?"

"I don't know," I told him.

"Should we call the doctor?"

"Probably," I said.

I dialed the off-hours number for the perinatologists. The answering service told me Dr. Mahone was on call for the weekend and would phone me right back. The phone rang just a couple of minutes later.

When I described the pain the doctor said, "I don't know whether or not you're having contractions. It could be contractions at this stage, and just not feel like it. But if we get you on a fetal heart monitor we'll be able to tell for sure. We need to know, because we certainly don't want you going into labor this early. You better come right in to the hospital. I'll meet you there and we'll check things out. How long will it take you?"

"About thirty minutes," I said.

"I'll see you then," she promised, and I hung up.

"Dr. Mahone thinks we need to go to the hospital," I told Kenny, who'd already figured out that much from listening to my end of the conversation.

"What does she think is the problem?"

"She doesn't know," I said. "But we can't afford to start labor now. She wants to see me to rule out contractions."

"Contractions?" I could see that thought alarmed Kenny. "Why would contractions begin now? When did all this start?"

When I explained I'd been sitting at the dining room table making hamburgers Kenny registered surprise, then exasperation.

"I knew this was going to happen," Kenny told me. "It's because you had your family over. Every time we plan something, you go and do something else!"

As if it were my fault! As if I wanted to upset our party plans and deliberately spoil the entire family celebration! As if I didn't feel bad enough about everything already!

My initial inclination was to snap back at Kenny and defend myself. But I stopped because I realized, *He's not really upset at me as much as he's upset about me. He's worried!*

Kenny

Bobbi was right. I did feel incredibly frustrated about having our plans disrupted at the last minute. But I was more worried than anything else.

"Let's go then!" I said, taking Bobbi's arm and helping her walk through the house. "We're off to the hospital," I announced to the gathering family in our backyard as I helped Bobbi out the kitchen door, across the deck, and down the steps toward our car.

"Let me move my car so you can get out. Then I'll ride with you," Bobbi's mom insisted. Peggy hurried to get her keys and backed the Hepworth's car out onto the street. I had Bobbi reclining in the front seat by that time, closed her door, and hurried around to the driver's side.

"Don't worry! We'll take care of Mikayla," Bobbi's sister Barbara called out.

The moment the Oldsmobile's engine turned over, I shifted into reverse and began backing out of the gravel driveway. Bobbi's extended family watched and waved as Bobbi tried to fight back her tears. The celebration would have to go on without us.

Thirty seconds later we crossed the bridge out of Carlisle and headed toward Des Moines as fast as I felt safe driving. "You okay, dearie?" I asked Bobbi who was lying back in her seat with her eyes closed.

"Yeah," she replied softly. "The pain seems to have eased up a little."

As glad as I was to hear that, and as much as I appreciated Bobbi's calm, matter-of-fact manner, my own heart was pounding. I couldn't help wondering, *What is going on here, Lord?* I prayed silently as I drove, *Please protect Bobbi and the babies!* And I was thinking, *How many times are we going to have to race to the hospital before this pregnancy is over? I don't know how many more of these crises I can handle.*

Fifteen minutes after we left home we were almost in downtown Des Moines when Bobbi suddenly sat up and asked, "Where's Mom? She wanted to come with us."

Oops! Peggy had been moving her car when I'd hurriedly backed out of the driveway. "I forgot all about her," I said.

"That's all right," Bobbi assured me.

I knew my mother-in-law would forgive me. And I might even be able to convince her I didn't leave her behind on purpose. I really didn't! Even though I must admit this time was a less stressful drive to the hospital without Peggy insisting I drive faster and run every red light and stop sign in Des Moines.

Bobbi

When Kenny helped me into the emergency room, the first thing the receptionist at the admissions desk asked was if my water had broken. She obviously thought from the looks of me that I was at full term. I told her no and explained that we'd called ahead and Dr. Mahone was expecting us. She took my name, made a quick phone call, and then told us we were to go on up to Labor and Delivery. "We'll get someone to take you right away."

We didn't have to wait long for an aide with a wheelchair to arrive. On the elevator to the fourth floor the orderly tried to make conversation. "Is this your first, honey?"

"No, we've got an eighteen-month-old little girl."

"Then you've been through this before."

Not exactly, I thought.

"How far apart are your contractions?"

"Oh, I'm not in labor," I told her. *At least I hope not.* "I'm only in my seventeenth week."

I saw the look of surprise in her eyes as she glanced down at my stomach. "Well," she said, "second babies are always bigger. Mine was!"

I didn't even tell her I was carrying seven.

As soon as we reached the labor and delivery unit, I was hooked up to a fetal heart monitor. Then we waited.

At one point a nurse walked into the room to check on me and to look at the monitor. While we waited, Kenny turned on the television and we watched the movie *The Poseidon Adventure*, and tried not to worry.

Dr. Mahone reassured us a little when she arrived, reviewed the readings of the fetal heart monitor, and said, "You don't seem to be in active labor."

Finally, some good news.

"But I want to conduct a complete physical and then do an ultrasound to make sure there's nothing new we need to be concerned about."

"Your cervix hasn't changed significantly since I first examined you," she said during the internal exam.

More good news.

The doctor pulled a tape from her jacket pocket and took a measurement of my abdomen. Draping her tape measure from the top of my pelvic bone up and over my abdomen to the base of my sternum, she stretched the tape tight and squinted at the numbers. When she announced, "Thirty-nine centimeters!" I decided I needed to forgive anyone who looked at me and just assumed I was about to deliver. Thirty-nine centimeters was a normal fundal height measurement—for women who were nine months along. *If I'm thirty-nine centimeters at seventeen weeks, just how big am I going to get?*

"I'm a little concerned about that," Dr. Mahone said. "But let's get that ultrasound to make sure there's nothing else."

Kenny

I wasn't nearly as familiar with ultrasound procedure as Bobbi was by this point. I had trouble telling exactly what the screen was showing at any given moment. But I realized Bobbi was counting heartbeats right along with the technician and the doctor. "Five . . . six . . . seven."

Still seven! Thank You, Lord!

"The babies themselves look good," the doctor confirmed. She asked Bobbi, "Are you still experiencing the pain you were when you first called?"

Bobbi shook her head. "I'm feeling much better."

Dr. Drake nodded and smiled reassuringly. "If it was contractions, you're not having them now. And that's good because these babies couldn't make it yet."

"What would have caused the pain?" Bobbi asked.

The doctor shrugged and smiled again. "We may never know. The important thing is that the babies are all still fine." She paused. "I am a little concerned that you are already at thirty-nine centimeters. And I think the ultrasound offers an explanation. You are accumulating an excessive amount of fluid."

She went on to explain that the ultrasound indicated each of the babies had upward of seven cubic centimeters of amniotic fluid in his or her sac, about twice the fluid required at this stage of the pregnancy. While that amount wasn't a problem for the babies and wouldn't have been a troublesome development if Bobbi had been carrying a single baby, double the amount of necessary fluid, times seven, was a lot of excess fluid.

"Your uterus is only going to stretch so far," she told Bobbi. "At this rate, we'll never get you to where you need to be for the babies to survive the birth. If everything keeps growing at this rate you'll have to deliver too early or your uterus might even rupture. So we've got to do something about the excess fluid."

"How will you do that?" Bobbi asked.

"We're going to put you on a medication called Indocin. It's an anti-inflammatory drug most commonly prescribed for people with arthritis because it reduces the fluid that causes swelling. It's also used frequently in the case of multiple pregnancies with no known adverse effects. If it works like it's supposed to, it will decrease the present fluid and slow the increase in fluid as the pregnancy progresses.

"It may take a little time to take effect, so I'm giving you a prescription to take home with you to start taking immediately."

"When can we go home then?" I asked.

"I want Bobbi to stay another hour or two for observation—just as a precaution. Then you can go home. Make sure she takes it especially easy this evening, and we'll see her again at the office tomorrow for her regular weekly checkup."

That was the best news I'd heard all day!

Bobbi

"When you get home I want you to go straight to bed and stay there," the doctor instructed me.

I nodded obediently.

I was feeling very grateful to be going home and that the babies were safe. The doctor never asked what I was doing when the pain started that morning. If she hadn't asked, I wasn't about to tell. I didn't want to be scolded for getting up to make hamburger patties.

By the time we got back to Carlisle that evening, our backyard was empty, the picnic was long over, and my family had dispersed. But they were all anxiously waiting for word and rejoiced at our good report.

Mom drove me to Des Moines for my regularly scheduled doctor's appointment the next morning. One of the nurses I'd gotten to know over the preceding weeks came into the room while I was waiting for the doctor. "I just now heard you had a little scare yesterday morning."

I nodded. "We came into the hospital. But everything seemed to be okay, so Dr. Mahone sent me home."

The nurse smiled. "I wanted to tell you," she said. "Yesterday at my church they listed people we needed to pray for. Then they asked if anyone had an unspoken prayer request. I thought of you. So I raised my hand; you were my unnamed prayer request yesterday. I'd never done that before. At the time I had no idea why you came to mind or why I'd felt compelled to ask special prayer for you. But I came in this morning and found out you were rushed to the hospital yesterday. Now I know why God wanted me to request that prayer. Because you needed it."

I got goose bumps and felt all choked up by the time she finished. But I did manage to thank her for her prayers.

I had a more extensive ultrasound that visit—the second in the series of anatomy scans to check out the babies' development. This was the week for Babies D and E. We learned Baby D was a girl and E was another boy. Like the first three we'd looked at the previous week, both seemed to be perfect. No developmental abnormalities or anatomical problems at all. Dr. Mahone was thrilled.

At the very first appointment with our neonatologists back in June, Dr. Mahone had cautioned us to plan on me going into the hospital at least by the twentieth week, if not sooner. That time was fast approaching. I'd looked at a calendar to see that the twenty-week mark fell right in the middle of Labor Day weekend. So during this August 19 appointment I pointed that out to Dr. Mahone and asked if it would be possible to wait until the Tuesday after Labor Day to be admitted to the hospital. That way I could be home with Mikayla and Kenny over his long weekend off.

"Is there a particular reason why you want to be admitted to the hospital at twenty weeks?" Dr. Mahone asked.

"I didn't think I had a choice." I reminded her about what she'd said during our first visit.

She smiled and nodded her head. "I did say that. And to tell you the truth, I never expected you to make it that far. We have to base our expectations on past experience. We follow a proto-col based on other multiple birth mothers we've worked with. But we're in brand-new territory here. There is no protocol for seven babies. So we haven't known what to expect.

"The fact is I can't remember any high-risk multiple birth mothers we've ever had—even with twins or triplets—who haven't spent at least one night in the hospital by this seventeen-week point in the pregnancy. You're doing so well that I don't think there's any reason for you to have to go into the hospital until there's some new indication that you need to. And at this point, I couldn't begin to predict when that would have to be. You've already defied all the expectations.

"You and the babies are doing so well it's amazing. Dr. Drake and I can't take any credit. Clearly, God is at work in this pregnancy!"

For the second time that day I felt goose bumps. I wondered if Dr. Mahone knew what the nurse had told me about praying for me the day before.

I went home from the doctor's office feeling more encouraged than I'd felt since we first learned we were expecting septuplets. I couldn't wait to tell Kenny about the appointment. That we had another girl and boy. And what the nurse and the doctor had said.

From the beginning we'd believed that God was in this preg-nancy. Now even the medical people were sensing it.

Nine

A B C A B C A

It Was No Secret

Kenny

Up to this time, the news media had somehow remained unaware of us and our situation. And we appreciated people like the nurse who requested prayer for us—but kept our names out of it. We weren't really trying to keep our pregnancy a secret. In fact, a large number of people knew that a couple in Iowa were expecting seven babies. And a lot of those people were praying for us by our names. Only the news media seemed to be in the dark.

Initially we had shared our news with just our families because we weren't ready to talk to other people. But in mid-June, at a Wednesday night church youth group meeting, my fifteen-year-old brother, Matt, spilled the beans when he said: "I'd like to ask prayer for my sister-in-law, Bobbi, who is expecting seven babies."

None of the youth group knew what to say or whether to even believe him. But my fourteen-year-old sister, Alisha, was just about ready to strangle Matt. When he saw the daggers in his sister's eyes he exclaimed, "What?!"

"You were *not* supposed to tell!" Alisha mouthed at him.

"I didn't know . . . I thought . . . well, it's too late now," Matt sputtered.

At home later that evening, our pastor's son, a member of the youth group and a friend of Matt's, asked his father: "Dad, is it true? That Bobbi McCaughey is pregnant with seven babies?"

Pastor Brown confirmed it. "Yes, son, that is true. But how did you find out?" Once he heard the story, he asked his son not to repeat a word of it. But Matt had been right. It was too late now.

Dad called me that evening to report what had happened. Alisha had filled him in on Matt's blunder. My brother felt terrible. But we all agreed that "it was going to get out sooner or later." The very next day our pastor received a phone call from a woman in our church asking him if he could confirm what she'd heard at work. Was Bobbi pregnant with seven babies? So, Pastor called us.

"The cat seems to already be out of the bag," he told us. "Perhaps the best thing now is to take a direct approach. Kenny, would you be willing to make an announcement in church next Sunday?

"If you just go ahead and tell people, that will cut down on people speculating and asking each other questions. You can get the story straight.

"And if some church members hear the gossip now, and others find out later, people are going to get their feelings hurt. If we go ahead and tell everyone, we can keep that from happening."

Bobbi and I agreed and the three of us decided the best time would be to tell the congregation at the end of the morning wor-ship service the next Sunday. So after Pastor Brown finished his sermon and before the benediction, he said, "Now, I'd like for Kenny McCaughey to come up. He has something to tell us."

I was nervous, getting up in front of everyone at church. We were sitting near the back, so the church aisle seemed kind of long, as I walked up it that morning. When I got to the front, I turned and faced our church family.

"I know you are wondering what I am doing up here this morning. I want to thank you for praying for us. You prayed for us when Bobbi couldn't get pregnant. And you rejoiced with us when we were pregnant with Mikayla. Some of you have been praying for us, knowing that we've wanted another child. I'm asking you to pray for us again.

"There is a rumor floating around about our family. I am here to tell you that, yes, it is true. We are expecting not two, not three, not even four babies. We are pregnant with seven babies."

I could hear the surprised exclamations, the *ohs!* and the *ahhs!* rumble throughout the sanctuary.

Pastor stepped back up to the microphone and added, "We ask that you keep this news within the church, among ourselves. Bobbi and Kenny wanted you to know, but it's not public information yet."

Afterward, some members of the church came over to talk to us, with words of encouragement:

"We'll be praying for you."

"What a wonderful blessing!"

"Congratulations!"

Others didn't say much. I don't think they knew what to say.

Bobbi

At the end of that service, Mikayla and I headed for the nursery to change her diaper. The nursery worker, who hadn't been in church to hear the announcement, came over to me and asked, "Is it true what I've heard? That you and Kenny are expecting five babies?"

"No." I laughed. "We're expecting *seven* babies."

"Oh!" said the woman. Her immediate response was, "You and Kenny are the two who can do it!" I was glad she had such confidence in us.

Our church family did a wonderful job of encouraging us and protecting our privacy. But too many people knew about our news for us to hope to keep it secret for long.

Kenny

Around the time we told our friends at church, I told my fellow workers at Wright Chevrolet.

After that first ultrasound clearly showing seven babies, Bobbi brought ultrasound pictures home for me to see. I took those photos with me to show my friends at work. The news spread quickly around the dealership, "The McCaugheys are expecting seven babies! And Kenny has some pictures to prove it."

Reaction was mixed from coworkers, neighbors, and friends around town who heard our news. A number of people questioned how we would ever be able to afford seven babies. Some people went so far as to ask, "Isn't there something you can do to reduce the number of babies?" I remember at least one person suggesting, "You just need to get rid of some of them!" But a lot of others merely grinned and shook their heads in amazement as they said, "Congratulations!"

Before long, the news had spread far beyond the city limits of Carlisle. Pastor Brown sent a letter to all our sister congregations in the GARBC (General Association of Regular Baptist Churches) throughout Iowa. Using only our first names he said:

We are writing to communicate with you regarding a young couple in our church whom God has blessed with seven unborn babies all at once. Kenny and Bobbi have been very active in our church ministry in youth, music, and teaching, and are faithful in attendance to the Lord's house. They already have one child, a 19-month old, but with the addition of seven more their quiver will certainly be full. Some have suggested selective abortion, yet, due to their faith in the omnipotent God, that option was never one they would consider.

Bobbi has just completed her 18th week of pregnancy at the time of this letter. She is required to stay lying down all but one hour per day, every day, and is to consume 4,000 calories per day. She is checked by her doctor each week and may need to enter the hospital at 20 weeks. The babies will continue to stay in the hospital until they reach the original due date of mid-January, no matter when they are born, and of course that could be much longer with any complications.

As a church family, we are asking for your unceasing prayer support for Kenny and Bobbi. Currently our church family is providing meals and laundry care. We are also in the process of determining what we as a church will be able to do financially to help with future added expenses. However, as time progresses we may need your assistance for items such as transportation, expanding housing, and 7 of everything, you can only imagine. We will keep you posted as to the progress.

If you have knowledge of governmental or private agencies that may be contacted for assistance please let Pastor Brown know at . . . [and gave the street and E-mail addresses for our church].

Our news was spreading. But with it, so was our prayer support.

Bobbi

My brothers and sisters and other family members had already shared our prayer request with their churches in nearby communities. So the members of those churches knew and were praying for us. After my grandfather passed along our good news to my Uncle Henry in Canada we soon learned that his church was praying for us and for the safety of the babies. One of my cousins told her school about us. So the students in a Christian school in Canada were also praying for Kenny, Mikayla, and me . . . and the babies.

A little later Pastor Brown's letter went nationwide by E-mail to all the GARBC churches in this country and in Canada. Yet, amazingly, the news media still remained unaware of us.

Kenny

We were grateful for the outpouring of prayer and support we received from our church, our community, and people across North America. We were also grateful that, while dealing with the ups and downs of Bobbi's pregnancy, we did not also have to deal with news reporters or criticisms from strangers.

Bobbi

One of the major high points of the summer for me was described in my journal for August 26:

Today is the last of the anatomy scans. I am so glad! My back has begun hurting so bad I can hardly lie still. Today took a little longer, because we had to measure the fluid around each one.

The last two babies look as good as the first five. And they are both boys. So we have 3 girls and 4 boys. Kenny was glad because (with Mikayla) that will make things even.

The good news kept coming. For so long I had assumed that I would have to be in the hospital by Labor Day. But, much to my relief and joy, that holiday came and went without any major complications. We were now past the point when everyone had thought I would be hospitalized. Instead my journal entry on September 2 read:

> Today was a standard visit with the doctor. The ultrasound was just to check heart rates and measure the fluid. And then I had my cervix checked. Everything is still fine.

I was glad I wasn't in the hospital over the holiday. That was the weekend my parents moved. Ever since they'd moved to Iowa from Nevada to help take care of my grandmother, they had been living in the basement of my sister Barbara's home in Des Moines. But they'd finally found a house in Carlisle, just what they wanted, the right size and something they could afford, in the same block and just around the corner from us.

I couldn't really help with the move. I stayed at home, lying on our couch, while Kenny and my brothers spent much of the weekend hauling furniture and boxes. Later in the day on Monday, we went over to Kenny's dad's house for a Labor Day cookout.

At the doctor's appointment the following week we got more good news: The fluid around the babies was slowly going down. The Indocin was working! What a relief! And it seemed to be working evenly: The fluid had decreased about the same for each baby. The doctors, implying that was unusual, acted very pleased.

I was twenty weeks along now, that much closer to the twenty-four-week mark, the gestational age at which our doctors said our babies would have a fifty-fifty chance of survival. And I had made it another week without a crisis that put me in the hospital.

However, at the next doctor's appointment, the news was not so good. I'd had a glucose test at twelve weeks to determine if I had gestational diabetes—the type of diabetes that can occur during pregnancy. At that time my blood sugar had been fine. But now, when I took that test again at twenty-one weeks, my results were too high.

On Friday, September 1 2, I had to go into the hospital for a three-hour glucose test. Kenny dropped me off at the hospital a little after 7:00 A.M., before he went on to work. I was assigned to a room almost immediately. I hadn't been allowed to eat after midnight the night before, so I already felt starved. By the time I finished the test, it was after noon and I was so hungry I was almost sick. I was, after all, eating for eight. They brought me lunch as soon as the test was done.

By the time I'd finished eating, they had the results: I did indeed have gestational diabetes.

My main worry initially was for the fluid around our babies. I knew gestational diabetes can cause excess amniotic fluid. I was already on Indocin to reduce that fluid. And the medication had seemed to be working. *What if the diabetes complicates that?*

Dr. Drake came in and answered my questions. She told me that she thought we could control the diabetes with my diet.

And she did not expect it to cause the babies any significant problems.

Kenny called me while I was still at the hospital to ask for the test results. I gave him a report of all the doctor had told me.

Barbara picked me up at the end of the test to take me home.

A couple of days later, my mother drove me back to the hospital for diabetic training. This time I packed a bag, since I would need to stay for twenty-four hours.

During that time I learned to use a Glucometer to measure my blood sugar. I also received instruction on how to modify my eating habits with a high-carbohydrate and low-sugar diet. The doctor told me that I wouldn't need to use insulin unless the diet failed to control the diabetes.

Using the Glucometer meant that I had to prick my finger seven times a day: first thing in the morning, before and after each meal, and at bedtime. After a few weeks, when it was clear that the diet was working, I was able to cut back, testing myself with the Glucometer every other day. Even so, for a while, my fingers were always very sore.

While gestational diabetes certainly was not good news, it was still not enough to put me in the hospital, and that *was* good news. Kenny and Mikayla came to visit me that one night in the hospital. And the next morning, when he drove me home, I felt incredibly grateful to still be able to go home and be with my family.

Kenny

Each week, when Bobbi would visit the doctor and then come back home, was wonderful for us. Each week, when her mother would drive her in, I wondered if the exam would find something that meant she needed to be hospitalized. Every day she came back home felt like a special gift from God.

But we knew that couldn't last much longer.

Bobbi

Not long after I developed gestational diabetes, I received a letter that reminded me again just how fortunate we were. The letter was from a mother who had given birth to twins just seven months earlier. They had been born at twenty-five weeks—fifteen weeks premature. One of her babies had died. In the letter, this woman said that she had heard about our seven babies, and she wanted her letter to encourage us. She was letting us know she was praying for us. She told me I didn't need to answer her letter if I didn't want to. And I didn't write her back. But I appreciated knowing that she was praying for me.

At my doctor's visit on October 7, we checked heart rates and fluid levels and we measured the babies. I was twenty-four weeks along and the babies weighed in at:

Baby A (Kenny): 1 pound 12 ounces
Baby B (Natalie): 1 pound 10 ounces
Baby C (Alexis): 1 pound 7 ounces
Baby D (Kelsey): 1 pound 8 ounces
Baby E (Nathan): 1 pound 10 ounces
Baby F (Brandon): 1 pound 10 ounces
Baby G (Joel): 1 pound 12 ounces

The doctors were pleased that the babies' weights were so even—and so much higher than anyone expected them to be. Dr.

Drake told me that it was "Phenomenal!" that their weights were so consistent and so good.

In my journal that day, I wrote:

> So between all of them, I have 11 lbs. 4 oz. in there. No wonder I look and feel like a house.

This was the day that I started steroid shots—a fairly new but standard procedure for high-risk pregnancies. The steroids help the babies' lungs begin to develop earlier, a precaution that can make a crucial difference in a premature birth. The shots would also help prevent internal bleeding during and after delivery.

We got only one item of bad news that day, but it was serious: Baby D's amniotic fluid was low.

"She still has enough fluid for now," the doctors assured us. "The fluid is lower than we want, but it is not imminently life-threatening. However, that could change overnight. If her fluid goes any lower, she will be in immediate danger." This was hardly surprising. If anything, the doctors had expected this earlier. Indocin, the medicine I'd been taking for several weeks to prevent an excess of amniotic fluid, rarely works evenly in a multiple birth.

Dr. Mahone sat me down at the end of the appointment for a serious talk:

"We have reached a decision point. You and Kenny have a choice to make. I see three possibilities.

"The first is that you could stop taking Indocin. That should help Baby D. But the other six babies would probably begin gaining fluid again. If they gain too much fluid, you would go into labor or your uterus could rupture.

"At twenty-four weeks, the babies have a little more than a

fifty-fifty chance of surviving an emergency C-section. But the risk of long-term developmental problems in babies born at twenty-four weeks is very high. We need to reach that critical twenty-eight-week point in order for the babies to have a real fighting chance—not just for survival, but also for good health."

Dr. Mahone was clearly not comfortable with this first option. She continued:

"Or, the second possibility is this—you could keep taking the Indocin, return for your appointment next week, and just see what happens. But, in the meantime, if Baby D loses more fluid, her heart might stop beating.

"Option three is for you to be admitted to the hospital. You would keep taking Indocin, but we could monitor Baby D closely, taking an ultrasound every other day. If she continues to lose fluid, we could talk about what steps to take."

I had listened to all the choices with a sinking heart. "I'll have to talk this over with Kenny," I told the doctor.

My mom drove me home. We didn't talk much.

Kenny

That night, Bobbi and I lay in bed, talking over our options. Bobbi curled up, facing me in bed, and told me again everything the doctor had said to her. I stared up at the ceiling while I listened, trying to absorb all the information.

"Maybe we need to look at the bigger picture," Bobbi said when she finished her report of the doctor's visit. "If we deliver now, all the babies will suffer. Maybe we have to let this baby go, for the sake of the other six." I could hear the hurt in her voice, just mentioning that possibility.

As I had listened to Bobbi describe our possible choices, I had thought, *Lord, this is another test. What should we do?* By now I loved and wanted all seven babies. It broke my heart to think of letting even one of them go. But delivering all of them this early, for the sake of one, didn't seem like a good decision, either.

We had succeeded in defying all odds up to this point. Bobbi had even been able to stay home much longer than anyone had expected. But maybe now was the time for her to be hospitalized.

By the time Bobbi and I finished talking that night, we had decided that she would go into the hospital for the week, to let the doctors keep a close eye on Baby D. We felt that we needed to do everything we could to safeguard each one of our children.

"Lord, be gracious and let us keep this little one," I prayed before I finally went to sleep.

Bobbi

After Kenny had drifted off, I lay there and prayed for the life of our one endangered, precious baby.

As if to confirm that we had made the right choice about going to the hospital, God changed our plans that night. Just before midnight, before I could fall asleep, I began having contractions. They were not regular. But there were a lot of them and they were so strong, I had to use breathing techniques to get through them.

After an hour, we phoned Dr. Drake and told her about the contractions. She told us we needed to come in. She would call and tell the hospital we were coming.

We got up, dressed, and headed for the hospital, a few hours earlier than we had planned. Driving in I had mixed feelings. I was excited at the possibility that we might finally be able to see the babies. But I was also worried. I knew it would be better if we could hold off the birth for a while longer.

Ten

The Separation Begins

Bobbi

On October 8, I wrote in my journal:

Plans have changed a little. I'm still in the hospital today, I just got here a little earlier than planned. I came in last night around midnight—having contractions. So I was put on a monitor for an hour, but the contractions weren't consistent, so they weren't a problem. I did spend the night, though, and Kenny went on home. Now I'm in the hospital to stay until the babies come. This kind of makes it all seem real.

The day we'd learned about the fluid shortage for Baby D, while we had still been struggling with our decision over the three options Dr. Mahone had spelled out for us, we'd called our families and Pastor Brown to ask for prayer. We needed wisdom and guidance to make the right decision.

I believe God did guide us, confirming our decision by means of contractions that sent us to the hospital. Those contractions stopped during the night, but Baby D continued to need prayer.

We called Pastor and asked him to spread our prayer request through our church's prayer chain. That meant Pastor would call the church deacons, asking them to pray for our baby. And each deacon had a list of names that he would call, passing the word along. And each of those people would have someone else to call. Prayer requests in our church go out in this fashion every week.

What we now asked Pastor and our church friends to pray was very specific, "That Baby D's fluid level will return to normal, but that the fluid level for the other six babies won't go up."

Kenny

We also prayed all this would happen without having to change Bobbi's Indocin dosage, which had controlled the amount of fluid so well for seven weeks. We didn't want to do anything to jeopardize Bobbi or the other six babies.

We knew lots of people were praying. And we believed God could answer our prayers. But the speed of the response still surprised us.

On Thursday, just two days after we checked Bobbi into the hospital, the doctors ordered an ultrasound to get another look at what was happening. The ultrasound tech measured the fluid around each baby. When she got to Baby D, she said, "This is great! Her fluid is about twice what we measured on Tuesday!"

She continued to measure the rest of the babies. The fluid levels for the other six had stayed the same. No one had expected that to happen.

As soon as she was wheeled back to her room, Bobbi called me at work with the wonderful news. "Baby D's fluid level has doubled! She is back up out of the danger zone!" She went on to give me a full report.

Later in the day Dr. Mahone came by Bobbi's room. "This is amazing," she told her. "Baby D's fluid level has risen, but no one else's has gone up at all. We're out of danger for now." She didn't offer an explanation, but the doctor acted very pleased. "That means you can continue to take the Indocin."

Incredible! Whether or not the doctor could ever give a medical explanation, we knew what had happened. *Awe* is the only word that truly begins to describe what I felt. Awe that God really answered our prayers so quickly, so exactly.

I really had felt God was working in this pregnancy from the beginning. We both believed that. But some days, when I was feeling the stress of it all, that had been all too easy for me to forget. *Now You've proved once and for all that You are with us,* I told the Lord. *From now on I'm going to trust You without question. No more doubts. No more worrying.*

And I kept that vow . . . for at least a day or two. *Oh me of little faith!* I had a lot yet to learn.

Bobbi

At the end of that first week, Dr. Mahone came into my hospital room on her rounds and announced, "We need to talk, Bobbi. What are we going to do about your hospitalization?"

I wasn't sure exactly what she meant at first.

"We checked you in because we were worried about Baby D. Now that she's out of danger, you're doing so well that we don't have any specific medical reason to keep you here. You could leave if that's what you decide you want to do. But I'd really like you to stay for the remainder of the pregnancy.

"Not because I'm worried anything is wrong," she quickly assured me. "But so that if any problem develops, if anything unexpected does happen, you're already here where we can respond immediately. And you won't have a half-hour drive just to get here."

That made a lot of sense. But I wondered about our insurance. Would it cover my hospitalization without a specific medical reason?

"I already talked to your provider about coverage," Dr. Mahone went on. "I explained the situation. When I told them what I was recommending, they assured me your hospital costs would be covered if you stay."

"I want to talk it over with Kenny," I said to the doctor. But I thought I already knew what we would decide.

When we'd made our original decision to come to the hospital we were thinking "one week"—just to monitor Baby D. But after we'd checked in during the middle of the night with contractions, I pretty much resigned myself to being there for the duration. Even with Baby D's incredible turnaround, I hadn't wanted to get my hopes up that I'd be able to go back home.

The doctor's reasoning made a lot of sense to me. And to Kenny. "We've made it this far," he said. "We don't want to take any unnecessary chances." So I was definitely in the hospital to stay, and that felt like the right decision.

Both Kenny and I found great encouragement in that wonderful report on Baby D. We saw it as the most incredible and undeniable answer to prayer so far in the pregnancy. But I have to say that we sensed an equally impressive answer to prayer in the fact that I hadn't needed to enter the hospital until my twenty-fourth week.

For most of the summer twenty-four weeks had been the

"magic number." The doctors had told us, and everything I read confirmed, that twenty-four weeks was the point of development at which our babies would become "viable."

Before that point, there is little chance for any baby to survive outside the womb. At twenty-four weeks there is a slightly better than fifty-fifty chance of survival. It was still no sure thing by any means, but at least our babies now had a fighting chance to survive.

Of course, we realized those babies born at twenty-four weeks who do survive usually have severe, often permanent, health problems. We certainly didn't want the babies to be born yet, but it was still an emotionally rewarding milestone.

For so long I'd hoped and prayed, "Just let me make twenty-four weeks to give these babies a chance." And I'd reached the twenty-four-week mark days before I even needed to be admitted to the hospital—which was better than I, or certainly the doctors, had ever realistically hoped for. A huge answer to prayer.

At this point we had a new magic number in our sights—twenty-eight weeks. With today's improved technology, procedures, and medicine, doctors have been able to save more and more premature babies at earlier and earlier stages of development. Our doctors told us that preemies born at twenty-eight weeks had not merely a real chance of survival, but a very reasonable hope for good health and normal lives.

Still, we understood what the neonatal experts had found true for triplets, quads, and even quints wouldn't necessarily hold true in my case. No one knew what to expect with seven babies. There were no "experts" on septuplets because no one had ever given birth to septuplets who all survived—not in the entire history of the world.

And yet, I encouraged myself, *The experts hadn't expected me to make twenty-four weeks either and we've crossed that hurdle. I began to think, or at least to hope, Maybe, just maybe, with God's help, twenty-eight weeks is possible. Obviously every week improves the chances for our babies. We're talking only four weeks. I can do that!*

My faith got an unexpected boost one day during the second week in the hospital when Dr. Drake stopped by the room to talk to me alone. "I have to tell you something," she said, pulling a chair up beside my bed. "But you have to promise not to laugh."

I told her I wouldn't.

"This has never ever happened to me before," she said. She paused long enough that I could tell she felt awkward about whatever it was she had to say. Finally she continued. "I woke up in the middle of the night last night. I thought I heard a voice. It was telling me that you are going to be okay and all of your babies are going to make it.

"Up to this point I've just been hoping," she admitted. "But I haven't had any real peace that all seven babies could be born alive. Today, after last night . . . well . . . I no longer have any doubts.

"I don't know if that voice was God. Or if in my mind I was hearing my intellect finally agreeing with what my heart believed already. But I know something or someone told me these babies are going to be fine. And I needed to tell you that. I don't intend to tell anyone else; they'd probably just laugh at me anyway. But I wanted you to know."

Wow! Maybe Dr. Drake wasn't sure who was speaking to her. But I was. And I thanked Him for passing His encouraging message along through her.

Only four weeks. I can surely do that!

What I hadn't realized when I checked into the hospital was

that each successive week would seem longer than the last. "Only four weeks" would seem to be a lifetime. Because some days felt like an eternity.

Kenny

All summer we'd been anticipating the time Bobbi would go into the hospital to stay until the birth of the babies. First it looked as if that would happen at twenty weeks. When she passed that deadline, we started focusing even more on that twenty-fourth week. And yet, for what seemed like ages now, part of me had been dreading the day.

As thrilled as I felt that we'd passed the twenty-four-week mark, as glad as I was that we now had Bobbi where she could get constant care and immediate help if something went wrong, as certain as I'd been we'd made the right decision to come in when we did, the reality of her hospitalization proved to be even more difficult than I had imagined it could be.

Way back in June when the doctors prescribed complete bed rest I'd felt as if I turned into "Mr. Mom" overnight. While I had taken on added responsibility around home and with Mikayla, we'd received lots of volunteer help from family and friends. And the truth was, Bobbi still managed everything, seeing what needed to be done and taking the responsibility for *what* got done *when* around home—even if she couldn't actually do it.

But the day Bobbi went into the hospital it seemed like the whole weight of the world, at least the Bobbi-Kenny-and-Mikayla-McCaughey world, suddenly landed on my shoulders. Oh sure, I still had lots of wonderful help. Bobbi's sister Michele had dropped out of college for the semester so she could care for Mikayla during the days. Other family and neighbors helped out around the house. Church friends continued to bring big home-cooked meals every other day, just as they had been doing for months.

The big difference was that Bobbi was no longer at home coordinating our lives. The responsibility for making the hundreds of little, and not so little, decisions of daily life and living now fell hard on me.

I very quickly came to the realization that throughout five years of marriage I had taken Bobbi for granted. *Never again!* I promised myself and God.

Being the pessimist I am, I'd imagined the single-parent role would be tough—even for the short term. Turns out I was too optimistic!

The job was far tougher than I'd ever imagined. The basic logistics of daily family living (things like schedules, meals, housekeeping, laundry) proved a formidable challenge. But far more difficult were the twenty-four-hour-a-day parenting responsibilities of providing for the emotional and physical care of an active, demanding, needy twenty-one-month-old who was confused and upset by the sudden "loss" of her mother.

Our normally boisterous, easygoing, and uncommonly cheerful little girl very quickly turned into a demanding, cantankerous, terrible-two-year-old—some months before her actual second birthday. While the changes we saw in Mikayla were easily explained, given the months of stress and disruption to our family life, her uncharacteristic crying and fussiness, along with my inability to do a better job of meeting her obvious needs, often made me feel like an inadequate parent.

(It wouldn't be until some weeks later that Bobbi looked in Mikayla's mouth and counted five new teeth. "No wonder she was such a bear for you." Bobbi laughed. "On top of all the other difficult changes, she was teething big time!" But that explanation, intended to make me feel better, merely underlined my feelings of parental inadequacy. *My daughter cut five teeth at once? You'd think I would have noticed!*)

From the beginning of our marriage, and even before, I'd never doubted my love for Bobbi. I would have said I appreciated her. Yet I must confess that it wasn't until she went into the hospital that I truly realized how much more I *should* have appreciated her—not just as a mother to our daughter, but as my wife. How much I needed her. How much I would miss her. How lonely and empty our bed would feel each night I tried to go to sleep without her.

I knew it was even lonelier for Bobbi in the hospital. Away from home. Away from me. And away from Mikayla.

Bobbi

The worst part of the hospital experience, at least the hardest part that hit right away, was the terrible sense of separation. At first, when we'd been anticipating weeks of hospitalization, I think Kenny and I both imagined him driving into Des Moines every night with Mikayla to visit me. Now we quickly realized that coming every day was neither practical nor even possible.

Kenny did manage to come in at least every other evening when he got off work. And after lying alone in a hospital room all day I was always glad to see him.

The visits were never long enough though. And a relationship limited to bedside conversations in a sterile hospital room just didn't feel very satisfying or natural.

We talked on the phone several times every day. If he didn't call me for a few hours, I called him, so we communicated regularly.

We both knew we were still there for each other. Our love was still there. But it just wasn't the same as sharing a life.

I missed Kenny. But he is an adult. Kenny obviously understood. Mikayla didn't.

So while I hesitate to say I missed Mikayla *more* than I missed Kenny, the separation from her was certainly a lot harder. Having spent every hour of almost every day with her, having shared every joy of her twenty-one months of life, each day without seeing her, each day without holding her, seemed like cruel and unusual punishment.

Kenny brought Mikayla to see me a couple of times a week. But those visits were often more painful, more torturous, than the days without her. Sometimes when Kenny walked into the room carrying Mikayla, she would cling to him and not even want to give me a welcoming hug. Most days she much preferred exploring the room or playing alone on the floor over snuggling with me or sitting in my hospital bed even to read books.

I told myself, *It's a strange and frightening setting for a little girl.* Or, *She's angry and just paying me back for leaving her; she doesn't understand.* But I understood . . . that our relationship had definitely changed.

Of course I recognized that the circumstances pushing and pulling us apart were unavoidable. But understanding *why* it was happening didn't make it any less painful. Every time my little girl pulled away or refused to come to me, I felt my heart being ripped out.

That explains why, as much as I missed Mikayla and always wanted to see her, I think I enjoyed best the visits when Kenny came alone. Some evenings with just the two of us in the room, he'd climb up in the hospital bed alongside me and snuggle up against my backside. He'd drape an arm over me and we'd just lie there, not saying a word, enjoying being together. But then he'd eventually have to go home and I'd feel lonelier than ever.

I'd never imagined that a simple, temporary separation could be so horrible.

The boredom factor made the separation seem all the longer. While everyone else's life went on, my entire world had shrunk to the size of a hospital room. I tried to reach out by telephone, calling my sisters, my mom, and assorted friends every day. But there's a real shortage of scintillating news to share when your entire day's activities are limited to eating, sleeping, showering, and applying makeup.

Each day seemed like a longer version of the one before. Even the food got monotonous. The hospital served the same basic menu from week to week—every Monday the same choices, every Tuesday, and so on. For me it was even worse because my diabetic diet limited the choices.

I got so tired of baked chicken I persuaded Kenny to smuggle in McRib sandwiches from McDonalds. In fact, I complained so much about my diet that Kenny began bringing me whatever food church members delivered to the house. So at least on those evenings he came to visit we could share some good home-cooked meals together.

My sister Barbara did her part to relieve the monotony of my hospital routine by going into labor herself on October 18—just ten days after I'd been admitted. She called me that morning to say it had started. She phoned again just before they left home for the Iowa Methodist Medical Center.

I kept my door propped open so I'd be sure and see her when she arrived on the ward. And a few minutes later when I thought they'd had enough time to get to the hospital, I went and stood in the doorway to watch for them. I timed it right; within minutes

Neil wheeled her past my room and down the hall. Barbara called out to tell me her contractions were just two and a half minutes apart.

So I settled back in bed to pray for my sister and wait for word on her imminent delivery. When an hour passed and I hadn't heard I began to worry. *Her contractions were only two and a half minutes apart. This is her third baby. Something must be wrong. She should have delivered by now.* Unable to wait any longer, I decided to check on Barbara myself.

I should have known better.

Eleven

Breaking News

Bobbi

*J*eased my bulky body out of bed and lumbered slowly, gingerly to the door of my room. I stuck my head out to take a peek up and down the hall. *The coast is clear.* I could see the closed door of Barbara's room just across the hall and down one from mine.

I'd managed maybe five short, cautious steps down the hall when the alarmed voice of a nurse boomed out from behind me: "May I help you with something?"

Busted.

"I was just going to check on my sister. She came in about an hour ago and I wanted to find out how her labor is going."

"Your sister is down in delivery right now. We'll let you know as soon as there is any news," she said rather sternly. "You need to get back to your own room and stay in bed."

Since it didn't look as though I had a choice, that's just what I did. But in between thinking about and praying for my sister, I couldn't help lamenting: *Why is it every time I decide to ignore medical orders, however good my reasons, I get caught?*

Just minutes later Neil hurried into my room to tell me I had a brand-new, 8 lb. 9 oz. niece—and that mother and daughter were doing well. In short order I got to see for myself. While Barbara waited for the staff to get her room ready for her, she had them push her wheelchair down the hall and into my room so I'd get to see and even hold little Bethany.

I snuggled that minutes-old newborn in my arms. Rejoicing with my sister and her husband, I longed for the time I could finally hold my own unborn children. And looking at my full-term, healthy niece, who seemed so small and helpless, I couldn't help wondering how much smaller and more helpless my own babies were going to seem.

Sharing that hospital experience with Barbara and Neil provided a special memory that will last us all a lifetime. But my sister went home with Bethany the very next day. Once that excitement was over, the only breaks in the lonely monotony were my regularly scheduled ultrasounds.

In fact the only journal entries I made for the next few weeks were on ultrasound days:

October 14—We're at 25 weeks and all is well. Baby D is holding her own as far as fluid goes. So there are still no worries . . .

October 21—Twenty-six weeks and all's well. Fluid and heart rates are wonderful. Just a couple more weeks and these babies can make an appearance. I can hardly wait. I'm starting to get very tired and weak. I want healthy babies, but I'm getting tired of waiting.

Ultrasounds became important weekly highlights for a variety of reasons. Not only did they break up the routine, they offered encouragement and hope and reassurance to dispel at least a little of my worry.

I have yet to meet one pregnant woman who wasn't plagued with anxiety at some point during her pregnancy. It happened to me with Mikayla. And I learned no matter how irrational and unfounded pregnancy worries might be, the anxiety is indeed very real.

What made for more worry with this pregnancy was knowing full well that multiple pregnancies multiply the potential problems. The anxiety was completely justified, which made those ultrasound reports all the more important.

From the beginning of this pregnancy I'd tried to steel myself for the worst. I never said anything to Kenny, or to anyone else, but I knew with seven babies the risk of catastrophic problems or horrible deformities was a very real possibility. The best hope for knowing ahead of time, and for relieving those fears, was those ultrasound tests.

So far everything the tests could tell us looked okay, and each week we could tell a little more.

Both halves of the brain continued to look normal in all seven babies. All hearts had four working chambers. All arms and legs were present and accounted for. None of the babies had cleft palates. Everything we could see looked fine.

But when pregnant women don't know of anything specific to worry about, they resort to worrying about the unknown. There's always plenty of that. And some of the most basic reassurances God graciously provides most pregnant women didn't work in my case.

There's always something comforting about feeling a baby's

movement inside you. The first time you feel it is a memorable milestone in any pregnancy. After that, every twist and turn, every kick in the ribs becomes a comforting indicator the baby is alive and well.

I'd felt the first movement back on July 14—long before the doctor thought it possible. I took that as a positive sign, just as I had every movement since. But unlike a single pregnancy where you know who is kicking, with seven I had only a general sensation of where the movement originated. I had no way of knowing who was doing what. That meant if one of our babies died, I'd have no way of knowing from the lack of movement.

I never approached one of those tests without wondering, *Are all seven going to be okay this time?*

Kenny

Of course I, too, worried about our babies' physical health. Trouble was, that wasn't my only worry. While I knew each passing week improved the odds of their survival, each week also brought us that much closer to actually having seven babies.

All those unanswered questions that had seemed so overwhelming back in the summer felt all the more pressing now. *How can we manage with seven babies? How will we afford a family of ten on my salary? What are we going to do for transportation? Where are we going to put them all in our house?*

Months earlier I had quickly reached the conclusion that since we had a God-size challenge there was little or nothing I could do. Except to try to believe it when I said, "We're just going to have to trust God to provide."

And I really had been able to believe that—at least enough to set aside those unanswered questions, try to take care of Mikayla and Bobbi, and constantly tell myself we'd keep trusting and cross that bridge when we came to it.

Now that "bridge" was right there in front of me. It was no longer enough to keep saying, "We'll just have to trust God to provide!" I wanted to know *how* God was going to provide.

I've never been the kind of person who can hide his feelings. People knew I was worried. My dad, Bobbi's father, and Pastor Brown all tried to reassure me. They each said pretty much the same thing.

"Kenny, you can believe God will provide even if you can't see how. When these babies are born there is going to be so much publicity, this story is going to be so big, that countless people are going to want to respond. 'How' God will provide is going to surprise you."

But any mention of publicity or reference to how "big" our story was going to be carried a whole new set of worries.

The doctors had warned us from the beginning that once the news got out, we'd have more publicity and interest than we'd want or ever hope to control. They advised us we didn't need that kind of distraction—that we should keep the details of our pregnancy as quiet as possible for as long as possible. And without any special effort on our part, that's what happened. Friends and neighbors and family simply respected our privacy. And the media didn't find out. Until Bobbi was in the hospital.

On October 10, Pastor Brown had received a phone call from Molly Cooney, a television reporter with KCCI, Channel 8, the local CBS affiliate in Des Moines. She wanted him to confirm a report that an Iowa Methodist Medical Center (IMMC) maternity patient, a member of his congregation, was expecting septuplets. Pastor asked where she'd heard that, but she wouldn't reveal her source. She did, however, indicate the reliability of her source and implied that she expected to easily confirm the story very soon with or without Pastor's help.

Pastor Brown wasn't about to speak for us, so he asked the reporter for a little time and promised to call her right back. He phoned Bobbi and me to discuss strategy before he returned her call.

Pastor told her, "I'm not about to lie to you. A member of our church is indeed in the hospital expecting septuplets." He also explained that the health of Bobbi and our babies was still very precarious, we were under a lot of stress, and the last thing we needed was the added strain of dealing with the media explosion that would occur if this story broke right now.

Molly Cooney and Pastor Brown talked for quite some time. She told him she not only respected our position and concerns, but as a mother she also understood the emotions involved and certainly empathized with Bobbi. For our sakes, she promised she would sit on the story as long as she possibly could. But she also made it clear she would run with the story if she caught wind that any other reporter was onto it.

Bobbi and I informed the hospital public relations department about Pastor's conversation with Molly Cooney. And our first publicity scare was just that easily defused.

The PR folks, like our doctors, had warned us that the story would be a big one when it did break. "But you've got plenty of other things to be thinking about," they told us. "We'll handle the media."

Neither Bobbi nor I could really believe there would be much media interest. We agreed to let the professionals in the hospital's public relations office handle anything that came up—if it came up. They promised not to say anything without first checking with us, and we agreed we wouldn't talk to any media who weren't cleared through them.

The phone call from Molly Cooney prompted Pastor Brown to make some contacts of his own. He had a lot more realistic picture than we did about what was ahead. He E-mailed a public relations man who had just retired from his college alma mater, asking further advice on how we should handle the coming publicity. He also queried a couple in California who had quintuplets, to get their input. He even called James Dobson's organization in Colorado, Focus on the Family. As a result of these contacts, Pastor came to the conclusion that we might need an official family spokesperson, in addition to the hospital public relations staff. That's why he called Marlys Popma from Des Moines, who was recommended by the Focus on the Family folks.

Marlys had only recently resigned as the political director of the Iowa Republican Party to become the executive director of the Iowa Family Policy Center, a Christian family advocacy group. Pastor thought Marlys could be of help to us, but we remained unconvinced.

As far as we were concerned, there never was any big secret. Hundreds of people in Carlisle, at the hospital, and around the country knew we were expecting seven babies. Yet we didn't hear anything from the media again for almost three weeks.

Why would we need a "family spokesperson"?

Bobbi

After my ultrasound on October 28, I wrote in my journal:

> Today we started another scan for weight. The babies are doing so well, it's hard to believe. We only did half, though,

because I can't stand to [lie still] any longer. Baby A—2 lb. 8 oz.
Baby B—2 lb. 3 oz. Baby C—2 lb. 4 oz. Baby D—2 lb. 5 oz.

They are all between the 48th and 60th percentile, which is
wonderful. And my cervix is still over 3 cm.

Last night I had two women come to visit me. They were
both mothers of multiples. It was neat to listen to their stories
and be able to get answers from someone who has been through
it. They also brought information on how to get a lot of free
things. That will come in handy.

The following day, October 29, I continued:

Today was the second half of the measuring process. The last
three babies are also doing very well. Baby E—2 lb. 2 oz. Baby
F—2 lb. 3 oz. Baby G—2 lb. 4 oz.

The weight of all the babies combined is 15 lb. 3 oz. Quite a
load to be carrying. My back has started to ache a lot more in the
past few days. I also got my belly measured—it [fundal height] is
55 cms. And I got weighed. I now weigh 180 and 3/4 lbs. I only
gained 1 and 3/4 lbs. in the last three weeks, but at least it was
something.

But all this was the least of what happened today . . .

The morning of the twenty-ninth the hospital public relations
office received a phone call from the local NBC station, Channel
13, wanting to know the name of the IMMC maternity patient
who was expecting seven babies. The hospital spokesperson said,
"You know we can't release the names of patients unless we're
authorized to do so."

"Then can you at least tell us the patient's condition?" the
reporter wanted to know.

"We can't possibly comment on a patient's status without a name."

Exasperated, the reporter said, "Then we'll get a name!" and hung up. Within thirty minutes Channel 13 had called our house and talked to Michele.

My sister called to warn me, but not before one of the hospital PR people came to my room to say, "Channel 13 is about to break the story on their noon news!" She asked how we wanted to handle it. I reminded her she needed to call Channel 8 and tell them they could go with the story. We owed Molly Cooney that much.

"They will certainly want interviews. What should we tell them?"

"Kenny and I agreed not to do any interviews for now. Your office can do all the talking. We're glad to let you handle it."

When she left I called Kenny at work to warn him. I filled him in on my discussion with the hospital PR folks. I indicated they were going to call Molly Cooney and handle any media inquiries just as we'd discussed earlier.

Kenny agreed there was no reason to change those plans. At least I thought he agreed.

The truth is, neither of us was prepared for what was about to happen. And I had an ultrasound test scheduled, so I missed the noon news that day to hear what was said.

No matter. All afternoon I took phone calls from friends and family who told me all about it.

Kenny

Not long after lunch, the first television news crew pulled onto the Wright Chevrolet lot. By mid-afternoon all the major networks had called wanting interviews and I could see two satellite trucks parked outside my office window. There they stayed, even after they were told that I wouldn't be giving any interviews. We had so much excitement and commotion in and around the dealership that afternoon no one could get much work done.

I didn't know what to do! The media people would *not* leave. I felt so terrible about the disruption that when a call from Channel 13 got through to my desk asking for a sixty-second live interview on their five o'clock news I made a desperate, spur-of-the-moment decision to talk with them. *If I give them something, maybe they'll go away and let everyone get back to work.*

I remember very little of the interview. I said yes, the news was true. We were expecting seven babies. And yes, we were very excited. I confirmed that Bobbi and the babies were doing fine so far. That we were over twenty-seven weeks now, but we didn't know when the babies would be born.

That's about all I recall from the very first television interview of my life—except for my incredible nervousness and thinking how weird it felt to be talking live on the phone to a newsman I could see on the television set there in our office.

By the time I finished answering Channel 13's questions I remembered our obligation to Molly Cooney. So I agreed to go outside and speak to Channel 8—on camera. Again I was thinking, *If I give them what they want, they'll go away and leave us alone.*

Looking back, I can hardly believe I was that naive.

ℬobbi

Kenny had called that afternoon when the trucks showed up. He'd been very agitated that they wouldn't leave when he said he wasn't going to be interviewed. The more calls he received, the

more news crews that showed up at the dealership, the more dis-
tressed Kenny became.

I tried to calm him down. But neither of us was prepared for
this sort of attention.

Since I'd missed the reports at noon, I was especially interested
to see what the evening broadcasts were going to say.

I clicked on the TV for the five o'clock news. Suddenly, looking out of the television screen in my hospital room was Kenny's
face. I couldn't believe my eyes. But there he was, standing in
front of Wright Chevrolet, talking live into a microphone. The
next thing I knew he was pulling out his billfold and extracting
a folded piece of paper from which he began to read. He blabbed
to the entire world the list of names we'd spent so many hours
trying to agree on. Four boys' names, three girls' names.

I could not believe my ears, either!

When that station cut away from the story, I switched to
another channel. And there was Kenny again.

About that time the phone beside my bed rang. When I picked
it up and said, "Hello," I recognized my father's voice. "What in
the world is that husband of yours doing? Have you seen him?"

"Yes, I've seen him. And I don't have a clue what he's thinking." *But first chance I have to get my hands on him, I'm gonna
find out!*

Twelve

Waiting Game

Kenny

The moment I walked through the door of Bobbi's hospital room that evening, I sensed some serious tension.

"Hi, dearie!" I said as I approached her bed to give her a kiss. She glared at me without answering.

"What's the matter?" I asked.

"You know what's wrong!"

I cringed. "It's the TV interview, isn't it?"

"We agreed not to talk!" Bobbi said. "Then I turn on the television and there you are. Telling the world everything you know—even what names we have picked out for the babies! What were you thinking?"

"I'm sorry!" I began. "But you should be in that situation and try not to tell them anything! They keep asking and keep asking. They wouldn't go away. I wasn't sure they would ever leave unless I told them something!"

I kept trying to talk my way out of the doghouse—to make

Bobbi understand how frustrated I'd been, how pressured I'd felt. "I didn't know what to do . . . I thought maybe if I talked, if I gave them something they'd leave us alone. I'm sorry. I know we agreed not to give interviews. I just thought it would help . . . I'm really sorry."

The harder I tried to explain and apologize, the more frustrated I felt. Before long I was pacing furiously around the room, saying, "I don't see how we're ever going to be able to cope with seven babies! We can't even deal with the media!"

It was not a pretty sight. I did calm down enough to talk when Pastor Brown came in and brought Marlys Popma to meet us. Together we tried to make a little sense of the day's developments. The hospital PR people also stopped in and joined the discussion.

I still had no idea how I would react to the media onslaught if it continued the next day. But before I went home that night, I did promise Bobbi, "No more interviews."

That was going to be one tough promise to keep.

The phones at home and at work never stopped ringing. We had fifteen media messages on our home answering machine by the time I got home from the office that first afternoon. The very next day I went out and got an unlisted phone number.

But that only relieved a little of the pressure at home. For the next few days calls and visitors practically swamped the dealership.

"Kenny, line one," would come over the office speaker.

"Kenny, line two," a moment later. Suddenly I was the star of a show I hadn't even agreed to appear in.

One camera crew traipsed through the front door and back into my office area uninvited. Any of my coworkers who were willing to talk, or who just couldn't figure out how to fend off the reporters, got interviewed, regardless of how little they knew about us or the pregnancy. At one point, I got so tired of the phone calls and visitors that I went into the rest room at the dealership and just hid out for a while.

One television producer from a national talk show hung around the dealership from opening to closing—day after day after day. He seemed friendly and nice, but very persistent. He was on a first-name basis with the entire sales staff by the second afternoon. He even made himself known to the mechanics back in the shop, where he particularly targeted my dad. He talked to anyone he could buttonhole, blatantly recruiting my coworkers to try to persuade me to give him an interview. I lost track of the number of friends who were soon saying, "You really ought to talk to him, Kenny. He's such a likable fellow. Why don't you do his show?"

I didn't blame them for liking the guy, but I'd learned my lesson. I wasn't about to break the no-statement promise I'd made to Bobbi.

Eventually, the string of unwelcome visitors became so routine at Wright Chevrolet that the management and staff of the dealership came up with a solution for regulating my instant celebrity status. Brooke, the receptionist, began screening all calls and visitors. She would buzz me to let me know who was on the line. If it was someone I knew, she'd put them through. If it was a reporter or even a name I didn't recognize, she would explain that I was unavailable and wasn't making any statements and maybe take a message.

I felt terrible about the inconvenience this caused everyone. But on the other hand I thought, *It isn't exactly my fault. And I can't do anything to help it.* The media soon learned they couldn't get anything out of me at work. But that didn't seem to stop them from trying.

Everyone who'd been telling us "This is going to be a big story!" was certainly right. On October 30, less than twenty-four hours after the story broke on television, we were front-page headline news in the *Des Moines Register*. The paper recounted some of what I had said to the television reporters the afternoon before—more than I remembered. Since our doctors were faithfully saying no to all media requests, the paper resorted to quoting a medical expert who had never seen us and knew nothing about our case. Under the banner headline, "Couple Waits for Seven Wonders," that first article said:

> Kenny and Bobbi McCaughey of Carlisle hope to soon become the parents of septuplets—seven babies—an event sure to attract worldwide attention because of its rarity. Bobbi McCaughey . . . is in the 28th week of her pregnancy, a fact that a specialist considers miraculous considering the number of fetuses . . .
>
> Dr. Norma Kirsch of Des Moines, who specializes in care of newborn babies, said it's extremely rare that seven fetuses survive this long in the womb. "To get triplets to 27 weeks is pretty good . . . But if they got her to 27 weeks," she said of Bobbi McCaughey, "it's a miracle."
>
> . . . "God gave us these kids," he (Kenny) said. "He wants us to raise them." . . . McCaughey also invoked his faith when asked how he and his wife will manage to raise seven babies.
>
> "We trust God will provide," he said. "We'll wait and see what happens."

Bobbi

On that first night, the day the news broke and Kenny talked to the media, I was furious and Kenny was a wreck by the time our first visitors, Pastor Brown and Marlys Popma, stopped by to talk about what had happened that afternoon. They broached the subject of our having a family spokesperson.

"The hospital public relations people will be looking out for the hospital's best interest," Marlys explained to us. "They will do everything they can to help you as long as you are in the hospital. But once you leave, their job will be done. And they cannot help you very much with the attention you receive away from the hospital.

"I think you are going to need someone long term, someone who is looking out for your best interest alone. It doesn't have to be me, but you need someone in your corner who is there for the long haul," she said.

The more Marlys talked, the more the idea of having a family spokesperson was beginning to appeal to Kenny. That seemed to be the way our pastor was leaning too.

Then, about a half hour after Pastor and Marlys arrived, Kim Waltman and Lynn Yontz, the public relations representatives for IMMC and Blank Children's Hospital, came in to talk with us. Kim and Lynn remained confident they could handle whatever media problems arose. They encouraged us to just let them handle the press.

They obviously hadn't been able to give Kenny the help he needed. But I was still not ready to take what seemed like such a big step against the hospital's wishes. *If they don't think we need a family spokesperson, maybe we don't—if we can just stick to our "no interview" strategy.*

Kim and Lynn came back to talk to me the next morning, October 30.

"We have to decide whether or not you are going to talk," they informed me.

"Well, *I* didn't talk," I told them.

Together, the PR people and I worked on a statement for them to release to the press. A statement we hoped would address the problem by appealing for a little consideration and reestablishing the ground rules. On Friday, October 31, we again made the top of the front page of the *Des Moines Register*. They had a family portrait of Kenny, Mikayla, and me, beside a headline that read:

The Mother's Statement

Thursday's statement from Bobbi McCaughey, who is at Iowa Methodist Medical Center pregnant with septuplets:

"Kenny and I appreciate everyone's interest in my pregnancy. Although we have chosen not to speak to the media at this time, we do want to thank people for their concern and wishes. Right now we are focused on this delivery and spending time as a family, which includes being with our 21-month old daughter. I am feeling fine and am in good spirits. I am receiving excellent care from my physicians and the hospital staff.

"We ask that the media be patient with us and let us experience this wonderful occasion without interruption. The hospital public relations department will be accepting all media calls on our behalf and we will not be granting any interviews prior to the birth. Kenny would also appreciate not receiving any calls or visitors at his workplace. Thank you for your understanding."

I desperately hoped that statement would be enough. That our fifteen minutes of fame would soon be over, someone would turn off the spotlight, and life could return to normal.

Kenny

The hospital did a good job keeping the media away from Bobbi. But the news reporters were definitely getting to me.

The second day after the news broke, a slew of reporters waited in front of Wright Chevrolet for me to get off work. I had to slip out the back door to evade them. But before I did, I called a neighbor and asked if any reporters were at the house. He went to his front window and told me he could see a satellite truck with lights and cameras parked on the street. But I had a Plan B in mind. I headed for Dad and Val's house. The media evidently hadn't figured out where they lived yet. I took the back streets, and hid out with Dad until after the evening news hour. Then I called my neighbor again. When he told me the truck had just pulled away, I made a mad dash for home, threw on a change of clothes, and raced for the hospital before any reporters returned. I felt like a fugitive!

Bobbi

For the second night in a row, we had a conference in my hospital room to talk about "the media problem." This time just my parents were there with us.

When Kenny told about sneaking out of work and having to hide for a while at his dad's house before he could go home, I could hear the distress in his voice. I began to think what people were saying was right: We needed help. *Maybe a family spokesperson isn't such a bad idea.*

Yet the hospital people remained convinced they could handle everything. I was receiving such good medical care at IMMC, I didn't want to rock the boat. But the past thirty-six hours had been a disaster. Kenny was a basket case. It was all too much! I finally broke down and cried as I told Kenny, "I feel like I'm in the middle of all this and I don't want to be."

So we talked once again about the advantages of enlisting Marlys's help. The IMMC public relations department could obviously handle local media and all the requests that came to the hospital. But Marlys had more experience with the national press and could help relieve the pressure away from the hospital. And Marlys had already received her board's permission to donate her time and services.

The more we talked the more it seemed we had nothing to lose, and maybe a lot to gain, by asking Marlys Popma to become our family spokesperson. Our parents also thought it would be a good idea. So we made the decision that night. "If Marlys is still willing to help, we should call her."

Marlys came to visit us again at the hospital a few days later. And we began planning a comprehensive strategy we hoped would keep the news media from destroying our lives.

With no "real news" to cover, the reporters scrambled for every tidbit they could dig up about our lives. The Des Moines paper even wrote stories about all the people wanting to do stories. Under a headline that declared, "World's Attention Turns to Des Moines" the *Register* said:

> The inquiries have come from as far away as Switzerland, Germany and Australia. Every journalist seems to be posing the same question: When is Bobbi McCaughey going to deliver?
>
> "We don't know when it is going to happen," said Kim Waltman, a spokesperson for Iowa Methodist Medical Center. Journalists from around the globe have fixed their eyes on the delivery ward of Des Moines' largest hospital . . .

As satellite trucks parked outside the hospital Thursday, staffers from television talk shows and tabloid newspapers were busy trying to lay claim to an exclusive story—an interview and photograph of the very expectant mother . . .

The hospital has been besieged—up to 20 calls per hour Thursday morning—with media requests. A London television station wants to film a documentary of the septuplets, Waltman said, while the *National Enquirer* and the "Maury Povich Show" also have requested details about the McCaughey family.

"A lot of the networks are sending crews to literally stake it out until something happens," Waltman said.

Hans Huebner, a reporter for ProSieben, a television station in Munich, Germany, said the septuplet story has worldwide interest. "Germany knows about this, and they are very interested in the story," Huebner said. "I'm going to wait a little and see what happens in the next few days."

Eric Faulkner of the *Daily Mail* in London agreed, "The fact that this lady is going to have seven babies, it's quite amazing isn't it?"

What amazed us was the sheer amount of attention we were suddenly getting. And despite the daily hospital statements, everyone kept demanding to know *when* the babies would be born. We had to laugh when Marlys told us about one reporter who called her for information. "You don't have to tell me the date," he conceded. "But do you think it will be long enough that I should get a cheaper hotel room?"

We were soon convinced we'd made the right decision by bringing in Marlys. She quickly proved she was not only up to the task, but had our interests at heart. With someone we trusted supervising the media hoopla, maybe we could concentrate again on what was important: preparing for the impending arrival of our seven babies.

Someone had given us a book on NICU (neonatal intensive care unit) babies. In the middle, a section of photographs showed premature babies at the various major points in development: 24, 28, 32, and 36 weeks. (A full-term baby reaches forty weeks.) When I first went into the hospital, our babies were at a gestational age of twenty-four weeks. I looked at the picture of the baby at twenty-four weeks in the book and thought, *This baby looks big! Our babies look exactly like this.*

Three weeks or so later, on a wheelchair ride back to my room from an ultrasound appointment at my doctors' office in an adjacent building, we detoured through the NICU. There I was able to see a real, live newborn baby who had been born at twenty-eight weeks. I was startled. He looked so fragile! And he had so many different things hooked up to him: a ventilator and IVs and such. Babies at twenty-eight weeks are such tiny beings. And our babies were still one week younger than he was.

Kenny

We took another, official tour of the NICU during the second week in November. This time I got to go along. All six grandparents came with us, so that we would all know what we could expect the babies to look like and to see how they would be cared for.

The NICU housed several newborn preemies at that time. They were incredibly *tiny*! And some of them had tubes and wires going everywhere.

As I looked around that unit I remembered how tiny Mikayla

Bobbi and Kenny on their wedding day, December 5, 1992

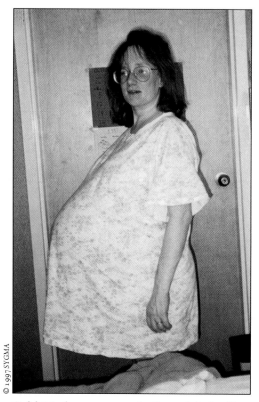

Bobbi in her room at the Iowa Methodist
Medical Center

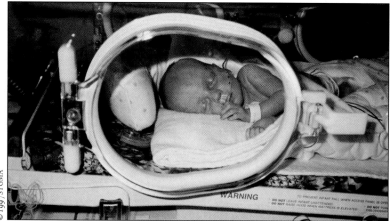

Alexis in an incubator

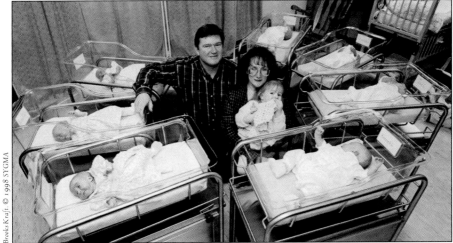

Kenny, Bobbi, and Mikayla with (*clockwise from bottom left*) Alexis, Natalie, Kelsey, Nathan, Brandon, Joel, and Kenny

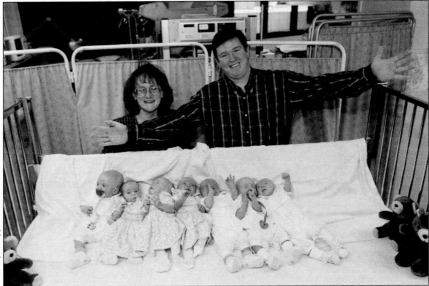

Bobbi and Kenny with (*left to right*) Kenny, Alexis, Natalie, Kelsey, Nathan, Brandon, and Joel

Mikayla, Kenny, Bobbi, and the Blank Children's Hospital team with (*clockwise from bottom left*) Kenny, Alexis, Natalie, Kelsey, Nathan, Brandon, and Joel

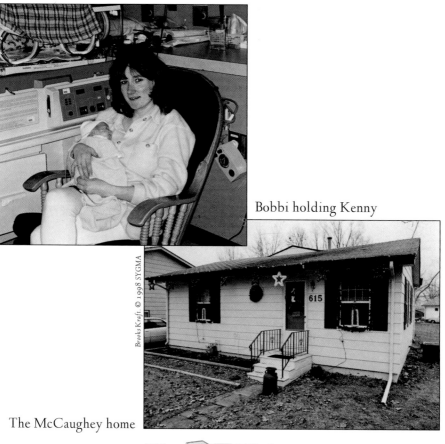

Bobbi holding Kenny

The McCaughey home

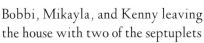

Kenny in the kitchen with one of the septuplets

Brooks Kraft © 1998 SYGMA

Kenny holding (*left*) Kelsey and (*right*) Alexis

Brooks Kraft © 1998 SYGMA

Bobbi, Mikayla, and Kenny leaving the house with two of the septuplets

Brooks Kraft © 1998 SYGMA

(*Right to left*) Pastor Robert Brown holding one of the septuplets, Kenny lying on the couch, Karen Heilman holding Joel, and Sherelyn Wilson holding one of the septuplets

(*Left to right*) Brandon, Mikayla, and Kenny

Kenny with (*left to right from top*) Nathan, Kelsey, Natalie, Brandon, and Kenny

Bobbi and Kenny with (*left to right*) Natalie, Alexis, Kelsey, Mikayla, Kenny, Brandon, Nathan, and Joel

At the Missionary Baptist Church in Carlisle: (*right to left*) Kenny with Kelsey, Bobbi with Alexis, Val McCaughey with Brandon, Ken McCaughey with Joel, Jason McCaughey, Kathy Addleman, and Dave Addleman

(*left to right*) Kenny, Joel, Brandon, Nathan, Alexis, Kelsey, Natalie, Kenny, and Bobbi

Kenny, Mikayla, and Bobbi

Bobbi and Kelsey
sharing a quiet
moment

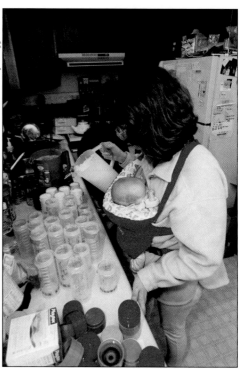

Bobbi and Alexis in the kitchen

Bobbi and Joel in the babies' room

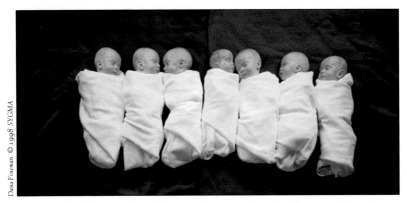

(Left to right) Brandon, Kenny, Kelsey, Alexis, Nathan, Natalie, and Joel

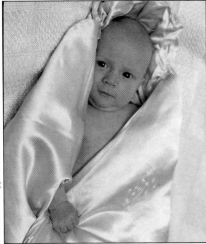

Kenneth Robert

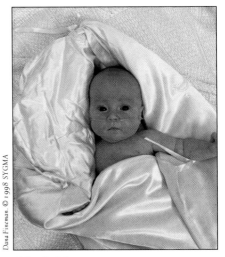

Alexis May

Natalie Sue

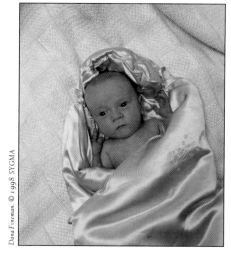

Nathan Roy

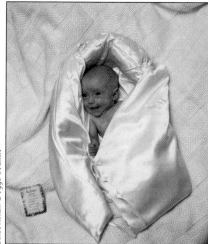

Kelsey Ann

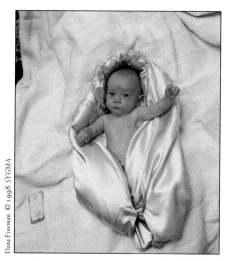

Joel Steven

Brandon James

(*Left to right*) Natalie, Nathan, Alexis, Kelsey, Brandon, Kenny, and Joel with workers at the site of their new home

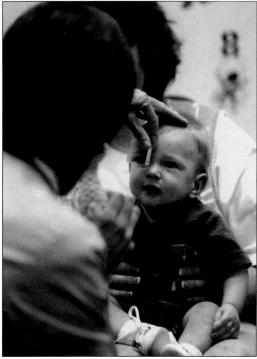

Dr. Jean Spencer doing a follow-up eye exam on Kenny as Bobbi looks on

(*clockwise from bottom*) Joel in the saucer, Natalie, Sue Subbert holding Kelsey, Judy Luke holding Alexis, Mikayla, Bobbi holding Nathan, and Kenny

Playtime on the floor: (*clockwise from bottom center*) Kelsey, Brandon, Marge Parlee feeding Nathan, and Kenny

The McCaughey children in their four-seat strollers: (*left to right*) Kelsey, Nathan, Alexis, Natalie, Michele (Bobbi's sister), Joel, Mikayla, Brandon, Kenny, and Bobbi

(*left to right*) Bobbi, Kenny, Brandon, Mikayla, and Joel

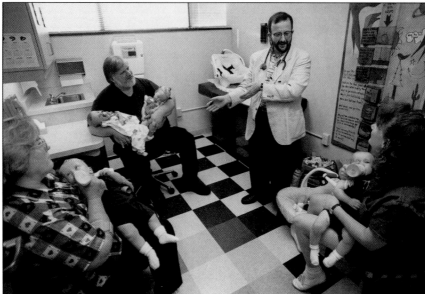

The septuplets' quarterly visit to the pediatrician: (*left to right*) Jeanne Bailey holding Nathan, Ken Bailey holding Alexis and Natalie, Dr. Pete Hetherington, and Bobbi holding Joel

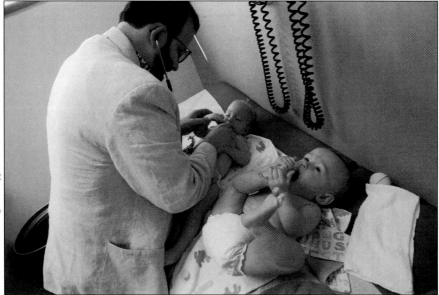

Dr. Hetherington examines (*left*) Natalie and (*right*) Joel at their nine-month checkup

had seemed when I first held her. Compared to some of these babies she had been absolutely gigantic.

I stood over the incubator of a little guy who'd been born at twenty-eight weeks and thought, *Oh my!* His scrawny little body was nothing but skin stretched over twiglike bones. *Our babies are even smaller than that.*

It wasn't until then that I think I finally grasped just how crucial time was. I thought, *If our babies are going to make it, they need every week, every day, we can possibly give them.*

Some of the premature babies we saw in the NICU that day were on special ventilators that blew six hundred puffs of oxygen per minute into the babies' lungs. That kept their immature lungs inflated, rather than inflating and deflating, which would be hard on them at this stage. But it also made the babies' entire bodies quiver and shake. They looked so . . . pitiful.

Watching those fragile babies, I couldn't help but worry about our children. *How small will they be? Will some of them be this sick? Our babies will come in here. And one or more of them might die in here.*

By this time, the hospital already had seven Ohio beds set aside for us, marked A through G—a whole row of the NICU just for our babies.

The doctors also gave us a play-by-play plan for what would happen on the day the babies were born. They had already held an orientation and planned a couple of practice drills for the forty to sixty medical personnel who would assist on the day of the birth. The hospital issued special beepers to all those who were on call and instructed them to be ready to respond at any time. The secret call sign would be "Code Seven." They warned everyone not to talk to anyone about the plans—not even their spouses.

No one was supposed to discuss it, even around the hospital among themselves.

We felt a little as if we were part of some top secret spy plot. I guess that was appropriate, because our doctors were carefully planning for B-day with all the care and attention to detail required of a massive military operation.

Thirteen

The Home Stretch

Kenny

*T*he plan was that Bobbi would be in one operating room, with a second OR set up next door as a holding room for the babies. As soon as each baby was born, he (or she) would be taken to the holding room where he would have his own four- or five-person medical team waiting for him. There the babies would be stabilized, intubated, and IVs would be started—whatever they needed immediately. Then they would each be transported, accompanied by their own medical team and armed security guards, through a series of blocked-off corridors and hallways to the NICU of the Blank Children's Hospital in a connected building.

In addition to preparing us and their medical staff for the births, the hospital was setting up necessary special security measures. As soon as the news story broke, they stationed a security guard outside the double doors of the labor and delivery ward. Signs were posted on the unit's doors, saying "No unauthorized admittance. All visitors must check in with the guard." Even people visiting other families had to be checked through.

As an additional precaution, hospital security took the number off the door to Bobbi's room and replaced it with a sign that said "Lounge." Visitors walking down the hallway of the labor and delivery unit wouldn't even realize Bobbi's room was a patient's room.

The hospital also completely removed Bobbi's name from the hospital computer system. That way no hacker could break into the system and pull the hospital's records—to find out where she was, or obtain any other information that might be used to endanger her or our babies.

We were still naive enough to think, *Surely all these precautions aren't really necessary. Are they?*

Bobbi

On November 2 we reached twenty-eight weeks. What a relief! Now we had a good chance of all of the babies living, perhaps without having any significant problems. Another amazing answer to prayer. Even the "expert" the newspaper quoted called it "a miracle."

As happy as I was to reach this point, I couldn't help wondering why in the world I'd been so sure I needed to check into the hospital at twenty-four weeks. *There hasn't been a crisis since. I should have just stayed home!*

Week twenty-eight also marked my twelfth week on Indocin, the drug I'd been taking to keep the babies' fluid down. Dr. Mahone told us she thought it was time to take me off that medication. Studies had been done that indicated Indocin is safe for pregnant women to take for up to ten weeks. But there are no studies that measure its safety after that. So Dr. Mahone wanted to take me off it and carefully monitor any changes.

She also told us, "You need to think about what you want to do now if one of the babies develops problems or shows signs of distress. Would you want to go ahead and deliver all of them immediately?"

Kenny

The twenty-eight-week mark was when I finally felt confident our kids were going to be alive and well. *It's definitely going to happen! God is allowing these babies to live. And if He can do that, against all the odds we've faced, I guess maybe I can trust God to provide for them after they are born just as well.* I began to concentrate more of my prayers on Bobbi and a safe delivery. I prayed for peace in whatever circumstance we had to face—not just now, but also down the road.

The newspaper coverage didn't help matters any. With no further statements from us, and no hard news to report from the hospital, reporters resorted to speculation. The financial picture seemed to hold special fascination. Newspapers interviewed medical, insurance, and financial planning experts regarding anticipated costs of everything from delivery to college diplomas. They estimated the bill for the pregnancy, birth, and post-birth care of our babies could run well over a half million dollars—just how high would depend on the health of the babies when they were born.

What the reporters didn't know, but I'd checked out early in the pregnancy, was that we had excellent medical insurance. We would have to pay our deductible, of course. But our policy had an out-of-pocket maximum, which meant the medical bills would not leave us with a staggering debt.

Articles about the ongoing cost of raising seven babies might have been more worrisome. The Des Moines paper talked to experts who estimated we'd have to spend over a thousand dollars a month just for diapers and formula. (That would be more than half my salary.) One financial planner projected college costs of several hundred thousand dollars for our children. Based on inflation and national averages ($145,000-plus to raise a child to age eighteen) the paper figured our non-college child-rearing costs would total more than a million dollars.

Two major factors kept me from panicking about the seemingly unsolvable financial challenges lying ahead of us. Factor one: I still clung to the conclusion I'd come to back in the summer—that this was a God-size problem. I didn't know what the Lord had in mind, I just knew He would have to take care of it. That confidence grew as much out of total desperation as it did any great supply of faith on my part. I had no option but to trust God because I knew beyond a doubt that the challenge was too big for me.

The second reason I didn't obsess over the ominous financial picture the experts saw looming in our future was that we had more immediate concerns. Thankfully, I didn't even have time to read those articles in the papers. I had all I could do taking care of Mikayla and worrying about the health of Bobbi and the babies.

For example, we had to consider the doctor's latest question for us: Now that the babies had reached a point where they all could survive the birth, what would we do if the next ultrasound showed any one of them had developed a problem? What if one baby stopped growing? Would we have an immediate cesarean section done and deliver all the babies, in order to save that one? Or would we sacrifice the one child, so that the others could keep growing stronger?

When we had faced this decision with Baby D, four weeks earlier, we had decided to keep the pregnancy going and pray for a miracle for the one baby who was in distress. A miracle that God had graciously given us.

But, now that we could expect the babies to do well, we changed our thinking. We decided that if one baby was in trouble, we would go for an immediate delivery. And we would trust God for a good outcome with all the babies.

Bobbi

Once we had made that choice, the medical strategy changed a little. Dr. Mahone ordered biophysicals on the babies twice a week—to monitor their progress. In these tests, the doctors observe the babies on the ultrasound screen, looking at fluid levels, heart rates, extremity movement, body movement, and breathing. Each baby had to have the right fluid level and heart rate and exhibit a minimum number of expected movements within a thirty-minute period, during which he could earn a total of eight points.

If any one of the babies failed this test twice in a row, he would be considered in distress. Should that happen, we would deliver all of the babies immediately.

We conducted the first of these tests on November 6. All seven babies scored a perfect 8.0.

That day, in my journal I wrote:

> I also had my fundal height measured. My stomach is now 58 cm big. (40 cm is the normal measurement for a full-term pregnancy.) And I measured it around. That's 53 inches. The nurses tell me I get bigger every day. My body is getting to the

point of being completely worn out. I can hardly stand long enough to take a shower. Then I have to sit for a while before I can curl my hair or put makeup on.

My legs are so weak. It's hard to turn over in bed. Everything is just getting more and more difficult.

So I'm praying that these babies will be born by the 19th of this month. I really want to be able to spend Thanksgiving at home and not stretched out in this bed. I miss being home with Kenny and Mikayla. It doesn't even feel like we're really a family anymore. I know that God is in charge, but I hope He sees fit to grant this request.

Kenny

The next ultrasound, done just a few days later, indicated that Bobbi was beginning to have contractions. Her uterus was so stretched that she couldn't feel them. But they were there, eleven or twelve each hour, some registering as strong contractions.

Dr. Mahone talked to us again. "While it would be okay for us to go ahead with the delivery any time now," she assured us, "every day we can put it off is better for the babies."

She wanted Bobbi to take Magsulfate, a muscle relaxant that stops labor contractions. We trusted her medical opinion. So Bobbi started the medicine immediately.

Bobbi

The first day I took Magsulfate, I did just fine. By the second day, though, this muscle relaxant had me so "relaxed" I could hardly function. Just opening my eyes required effort. It seemed more than I could do just to get up.

My bathroom was only a few feet away from my bed. But that day, just navigating my way to and from the toilet was a marathon project I had to plan and take in steps.

By the third day, I had adjusted some to the medication. But my muscles were sore all over from the effort I had made the day before. And I was on only half the normal dose.

Then the doctors started me on another medication, in conjunction with the Magsulfate. This medicine, Lasix, was a diuretic to help keep fluid out of my lungs, a side effect of the Magsulfate. Unfortunately, that meant I went to the bathroom more often than ever. Just at the point when I had no energy to move, I found myself trotting to the bathroom twice as often as before.

What bothered me the most was how emotional and out of control I felt on these medications. I cried more often than ever, and over less important things. Over everything, actually—and in front of everyone.

On Tuesday night, after I had started the Magsulfate, both Dr. Drake and Dr. Mahone came into my hospital room. When they asked me how I was doing, I broke down in tears in front of them, in spite of my best efforts not to. Instead of the alarm I expected, both smiled and said, "We're glad to see you finally expressing emotion. This is good. Let it all out." But I am not someone who is comfortable "letting it all out."

After five days on Magsulfate, my contractions had stopped. Another answer to prayer. The doctors took me off that medicine, but they decided I should begin taking Indocin again. Indocin also acts to prevent contractions, and wouldn't have such a negative effect on my emotions.

They also prescribed another round of steroids, to strengthen the babies' lungs and to prevent bleeding during delivery. Each set of steroid shots was effective for the next week to ten days.

Kenny and I were committed to sticking it out a little longer.

Kenny

We knew that each day we could hold out was that much better for the babies. That was our primary thinking. But we also had another reason for wanting to wait.

One local television station had made an "exclusive" announcement that we were scheduled to deliver on November 10. They cited an unnamed "inside source" of information.

We laughed when we heard that. Since neither we, nor the doctors, nor the hospital had any idea about when these babies were coming, we didn't know how their "inside source" could possibly know.

We determined that we had to get past that November 10 mark, so that they would not be right. We couldn't let them be right.

By the time the tenth came and went, the media frenzy had grown even bigger. On Friday, November 14, the *Des Moines Register* ran a front-page headline declaring, "Waiting Game Draws Even More Participants." Alongside a photo of reporters clustered in front of the hospital was an article that began:

> As Bobbi McCaughey's septuplet pregnancy stretches into the end of its 30th week, the worldwide hubbub around the expected births is also reaching a crescendo.
>
> Local and national television and radio programs have covered nearly every aspect of the expected event. And media representatives from around the world are calling Iowa Methodist Medical

Center, the McCaughey family spokeswoman and even local media daily for any whiff of news.

The crop of TV news satellite trucks parked in front of Iowa Methodist Medical Center has grown to nine. And "the Iowa septuplets," yet unborn, are showing up on World Wide Web pages and in chat rooms on the Internet . . .

Bobbi

Sunday morning, November 16, I woke to the sound of someone knocking on my hospital room door. I raised myself up to see two of my favorite nurses, dressed in green scrubs. They had stuffed as many pillows as they could under their gowns, in a futile attempt to look as pregnant as I was.

They sang and danced across my floor and around my bed, a song that went something like this: "It's thirty weeks today-ay-ay; we've made it to thirty weeks today!"

That's all I remember of the words. Because we all cracked up—laughing and laughing.

The hospital staff had done their best all along to keep my spirits up. One of these same two nurses had repeatedly offered to stop on her way to work to pick up some hair dye and nail polish. "Anytime you want, I can do your nails and dye your hair. A new color might perk you up!"

I never took her up on her offer. But she always made me smile.

The following Tuesday, the doctors called us and asked for a meeting to discuss our options. After a five-day course of the Magsulfate, followed by three days on Indocin, I'd not taken anything to prevent contractions for two days. And I still wasn't having contractions.

Yet, we all knew that it was just a matter of time.

Kenny

When Dr. Mahone stopped by Bobbi's room at the end of the day, Dad and Val were there. We told them to stay, that they were welcome to hear anything that was said.

Dr. Mahone explained that we had four options. (1) Bobbi could take Magsulfate again, to prevent contractions. (2) She could take the milder medication, Indocin, for the same purpose. With either of those options, she would take her medication until it no longer worked.

Option 3 was to take nothing, and just wait for contractions to start again. Or, (4) We could decide to have the babies now.

"You are way past twenty-eight weeks. We never dreamed we could get you to thirty weeks. We are thrilled to have gotten you this far. You can deliver anytime you want. It's up to you.

"I know that you'll want to discuss this. So I'll stay on this floor, seeing patients, until you've made your choice. Just send a nurse to find me." Then Dr. Mahone left us alone to consider our decision.

"What should we do?" I asked Bobbi.

Bobbi began weeping. "I cannot be pregnant *one more day*!"

"Then I think we ought to go ahead and do it," I told her. I didn't know how much longer she could stand feeling wacky and I could tell that she was maxed out, size-wise.

Bobbi sobbed as she asked Val what she thought.

"I think you are right. It's time to go ahead," Val replied.

Bobbi

Kenny hurried out to look for Dr. Mahone. Val reached for the phone and called my parents. I listened as she reported to them what the doctor had told us.

"Should we come up there?" my dad asked.

"I think you'd better," Val told him. Mom and Dad arrived a short time later. By then Kenny was back, without Dr. Mahone, who was busy with another patient.

We informed my parents, "We are thinking maybe the best course is to go ahead and have the babies."

"Why do you want to have the babies now?" my dad asked. I cried and couldn't get myself together enough to answer.

"Bobbi's just had it," Kenny explained. "She wants the babies now. She wants them here, so she can be home by Thanksgiving. She has just had it."

"That is a valid reason to make this decision," Dad assured us. "Bobbi's mental and emotional state affects the babies. That is something you ought to take into account. Why don't we pray about it."

I lay on my bed, with Kenny sitting beside me. My parents sat on the heat register by the window, and Kenny's dad and Val sat on the love seat across from my bed. And we prayed together. We asked God if this was the right choice to give us a sense of peace about it. And we asked Him to be in all that happened the next day.

When we finished, we were all in agreement. "Let's get this thing going!"

Kenny went back into the hall and asked a nurse to page Dr. Mahone. When she walked in he told her, "We've decided it's time to go. And we'd like to do it as early tomorrow morning as possible."

Dr. Mahone said, "I don't think we can do it in the morning. That's too fast. I have to make some calls to see when an OR will be open." With that she left for a few minutes. When she returned, she told us, "Okay, we're on for tomorrow. But the earliest we can schedule it will be noon."

We gave her the go-ahead for noon the next day, November 19—the date I had prayed for two weeks earlier.

Kenny

By the time we all left the hospital that night, it was after midnight. The nurse gave Bobbi a sleeping pill, since she would need her rest for the next day, and she went to sleep.

The entire drive home I kept thinking, *Tomorrow is the day! How will I let people know? Should I have Dad tell everyone at work? Tomorrow is the day! Lord, please be with us because tomorrow is the day.*

And He must have been with me, because, believe it or not, when I got home that night, I slept too.

Fourteen

Today's the Day

Kenny

Today's the day, I thought as I got up on the morning of November 19, showered, dressed, and ate breakfast. *Today is the day.* I packed my suitcase, since I'd be staying overnight at the hospital with Bobbi and the babies. Friends had volunteered to watch Mikayla for us that day, so our whole family would be free to come to the hospital. I drove alone into Des Moines that morning, thinking, *Today is the day!*

The game plan, according to the hospital security, was for me to come to the back of the hospital where they would help me sneak in. But when I arrived, no members of the press seemed to be around. On impulse, I decided to march right in the front doors. *If anyone spots me, I'll just keep walking. I'll just look straight ahead and ignore any questions.* I parked near the main entrance and nonchalantly walked toward the hospital. Fifteen satellite trucks staked out the front of the hospital, but no one stopped me or asked me a question. As far as I could tell, I wasn't recognized. I got there at 9:00 A.M. Maybe no one in the media expected me that early in the day.

I took the elevator up to Labor and Delivery, checked in with the guard, and went straight to Bobbi's room.

"Morning, dearie." I greeted her with a kiss.

"Well, here we are," she said. "Today's the day."

"Yup," I responded. "Today we finally get to see our family."

Bobbi

I remained a bit groggy from the effects of the sleeping pill when Kenny first arrived that morning. He was a welcome sight! His arrival meant we were ready to get this show on the road.

I showered and washed and dried my hair. By the time I finished and was ready to lie back down on my bed, I realized I was having contractions. When I'd had contractions nine days before, the ultrasound had picked them up. Although some had measured "strong," I had not been able to feel them. These contractions I could feel. And they felt like the ones I'd had with Mikayla. I didn't try to time them. What was the point? We were going to have these babies around noon, anyway. So I didn't mention them to anyone but Kenny.

Then our families began to arrive. By early that morning the word had gotten around: *Today's the day!* And everyone wanted to share it with us.

Kenny's dad and his wife, Val, Kenny's brother Matt and his sister Alisha arrived first. His mom and her husband, Dave, popped in to give us their blessing. My parents, with Michele and Dennis, stopped in. Barbara and Neil brought their baby daughter, Bethany. My brothers Bill and Pete, along with Pete's wife, Linda, were there too. Kenny's brother Jason brought

Grandma Marie. In addition to family, Pastor Brown and his wife, Ginny, came with Marlys Popma, our spokesperson.

As the people we loved came and went from my hospital room, we talked and laughed, excited that the day was finally here. My father took videos, documenting my record size, 60 cm in fundal height and 55 inches around.

And we prayed. With Kenny's family, Pastor prayed. With my family, Dad led the prayer. We asked the Lord for a safe delivery, for no complications, and most of all, for healthy babies.

I know the Bible tells us as Christians we should pray believing that God will answer our prayers. But as I prayed that morning, the believing came hard. I remembered the odds against us, how so few of the medical experts had thought that all seven babies would survive. Part of me still worried that when the doctors got into my womb, they would find one or more babies had died.

Today is the day, I thought. *I will find out if my fears are justified. I am more than ready to have the babies born. I want to see the answers to our prayers.*

Around 10:00 A.M., the anesthesiologist arrived, introduced himself, and talked to me about what would happen during delivery. He made sure I had no questions.

Kenny

Even before Bobbi and I woke up that morning, the members of the delivery team had begun to arrive at the hospital. Most had received phone calls the night before or early that morning, telling them, "Today's the day." Others, like the anesthesiologist, had learned after getting to the hospital that day. Altogether sixty-six doctors, nurses, and technicians, from fifteen hospital departments, were scurrying around, carrying out carefully laid plans that included, in addition to the medical preparations, walkie-talkies and cell phones, secret codes and color-coded badges.

Hospital security painted red lines on the floors of the OR hallways. Only the authorized personnel could cross those red lines.

Since the delivery would involve three rooms—the OR, a holding room, and the NICU—medical personnel in each location had walkie-talkies and cell phones to communicate with one another. IMMC had tried to think of everything. Everyone wanted this day to go off without a hitch.

Around 10:30 A.M. my dad and I got dressed in green scrubs, with our hair under those attractive, funky OR hats. Dad needed the scrubs because he was planning to videotape in the OR. I had worn my Reebok tennis shoes, thinking name-brand footwear would make me look more like one of the hospital doctors that day. I clowned around, modeling my "doctor" getup. The family laughed at how *cool* Dad and I looked in our surgical attire.

Laughter helped disguise the underlying tension we all sensed. The air seemed full of electricity that morning.

Even the news media soon realized, *Today is the day!* At least one of the local stations had been staking out my workplace all week. When I didn't show up as usual that morning, they knew.

The hospital public relations folks had suggested that when the day came we should let them issue a statement an hour before the birth. They handled that just as we'd planned. They called the waiting press into a large room set up for a press conference and informed about 150 reporters that, *Yes, today is the day.* The staff instructed the media, in no uncertain terms, that cameras would not be allowed elsewhere in the hospital and that the press would all be informed as soon as there was anything to report.

Bobbi

The whole hospital was abuzz with preparations. And my room was no exception.

At some point during that morning, Dr. Drake stopped by to check on me. I was sitting on the edge of my bed. "Good morning!" I said.

She asked me, "Are you ready?"

"As ready as I will ever be!"

She came over, placed her hands on my stomach, and commented, "You know that this day will change your life forever."

I nodded. As if I needed anyone to remind me.

"Are you having any contractions?" she asked.

"Yes, some," I confessed.

"Well, you are just going to have to wait until noon to have these babies. I haven't canceled my morning patients!"

Later, Dr. Mahone came in and asked me how I was feeling.

"Ready to go," I told her.

Dr. Mahone had already delivered one baby that morning. She went ahead and drew a line for the incision on my stomach: a long, vertical line, fifteen inches, from my pelvis to the top of my stomach. No bikini incision for this cesarean birth. Dr. Mahone would need room to take out seven babies as quickly and efficiently as possible.

Dr. Mahone had left my room before I realized that I hadn't told her about the contractions. I didn't call her back. It didn't matter. We were having our babies, regardless. *Today is the day, no matter what.*

Then, not long after eleven o'clock, a nurse arrived to prep me for delivery. She started an IV, got a catheter going, and took my blood pressure and temperature.

When she came into the room, the last of our families retired to the waiting room. It was time for the medical folks to begin their work. Plus Kenny and I needed some time alone.

We found out later we had so many visitors that morning they didn't all fit in the regular waiting room. So the hospital arranged for a larger, private room, equipped with snacks, drinks, and plenty of chairs, just for our friends and family.

By noon, the contractions grew strong enough that I was holding my breath. In some ways, that seemed comfortingly familiar. It meant this labor felt at least a little like the labor I'd had with Mikayla.

Shortly after noon a nurse and two security guards came to escort me down to the OR in the hospital basement. I climbed out of bed and walked to the wheelchair.

"Are you okay, dearie?" Kenny asked me as we started out the door.

I'm scared to death, I thought. *I have no idea what this will be like.* But I said, "Let's get this over with. I want to see our babies and be done with it."

The OR nurses obviously thought they would have to lift me onto the operating table and seemed surprised when I stood up, walked to the far side of the table, and got onto it by myself. I sat upright while one anesthesiologist put a second IV in my hand and another anesthesiologist worked on my back, inserting the epidural line. At some point, one of the IVs popped out and squirted blood. But that was soon stopped and taped down. Then I could lie down on the table.

A third IV was started, an arterial line that would enable me to receive a quick blood transfusion, if necessary. Someone else wrapped a cuff around my arm so they could monitor my blood pressure throughout the procedure. Other medical personnel situated me on the table so that the incision line was conveniently located for the doctor.

Someone put cuffs around my legs, pads that inflated and deflated during surgery to keep my circulation going. Someone else swabbed my stomach with alcohol and then Betadine. I felt like some sort of science experiment with a whole class of students anxiously hovering around and waiting for the dissection to begin.

Dr. Mahone arrived and repositioned me, to her satisfaction, on the table. I lay mostly on my back, turned slightly toward Dr. Drake. The anesthesiologist took a cold alcohol swab and tested my skin at various points on my stomach and feet, to see if I could feel anything. I couldn't, which meant the epidural was working.

Unfortunately, it worked almost too well. I felt numb all the way up to my chest. I already had trouble breathing when I lay down, with seven babies pressing up against my lungs. "May I have my head up higher, please?" I asked.

Someone got a section of an egg-crate mattress and put that under my head and shoulders. By the time I lay back on that, it compressed to about ¼ inch. *Folks,* I thought, *this isn't helping. I need my head higher!*

I also wanted to see. The surgical drape over my body had been strung up several inches above my chin, completely blocking my view. The greatest show of my life was about to start and I couldn't see a thing but green cloth. I would have to rely on Kenny and the anesthesiologist to tell me what was happening.

Because the doctors were ready to go.

Kenny

Suddenly, at 12:45 P.M., all the frantic preparations of the morning seemed to be done.

"Are we ready?" Dr. Mahone asked the room in general. Then she began the incision. So many people were crowded in the OR, all talking, that Dr. Drake finally commented, "We need this room to be quieter."

I was sitting by Bobbi's left shoulder and holding her hand. That position gave me a good view of the birth. I looked down at Bobbi's face during the incision. I didn't want to watch anyone cut on my wife. But once the uterus was open, I was captivated by the drama of the birth.

"Just a little prick," Dr. Mahone said, while she broke the first amniotic sac. Birth fluid shot up in a little fountain and a baby popped to the top.

"There's Baby A. It's a boy," Dr. Mahone announced. Someone said, "He's transverse." (That meant the baby was coming out laterally.)

As she lifted him out of Bobbi's womb, I introduced him to the whole OR crowd. "That's Kenneth Robert."

I held a slip of paper with a list of the names we had chosen. We wanted the first boy born to be named Kenneth, the second Nathan, the first girl, Alexis, and so forth. I wanted one of the first things each baby heard to be their dad saying their names.

Kenny's arms and legs were moving. He began breathing right away. As I looked at my new son, I thought, *He is so perfect. Smaller than Mikayla was, but bigger than I thought he would be. He is just beautiful!* I picked up the camera hanging around my neck, and took the first picture of our son.

A nurse standing near the door held up one finger to the window looking into the hallway, a signal that the first baby was born.

From behind a surgical mask, someone else commented, "He's a big one!" And throughout the operating room, I could hear a collective murmur of relief and approval.

As Dr. Drake clamped and cut the umbilical cord of our obviously healthy baby, she softly proclaimed, "God is great!"

She laid Kenneth in the arms of the neonatal transport nurse who, holding him level, his head away from her body, almost ran with him out of that OR and to the door of the other OR holding room twenty feet down the hall. Over the walkie-talkie the message went out, "We have a nice, pink baby boy," to let everyone know that he was breathing and showed no immediate problems.

A security guard stationed in the hallway accompanied each baby and nurse to the next-door OR. Inside that holding room, four or five medical personnel were hovering around an Ohio bed, waiting for our new son.

My prayers went down the hall with Kenneth. But I knew that my place was still in this OR with my wife.

As soon as Kenneth was born, Bobbi's uterus contracted and pushed another baby into position. Baby C popped to the top of Bobbi's womb next. Dr. Mahone pricked her sac and the birth fluids squirted up in a little fountain again. The people hovering over the table got splashed.

"It's a girl," Dr. Mahone said. "Also transverse," someone else commented. As Dr. Mahone lifted her up, I introduced her. "This is Alexis May." She began breathing and moving too. She was smaller than Kenneth had been, but still not as tiny as I'd feared.

Someone made the comment, "She looks good!"

But I thought, *She's beautiful!*

Again, as Dr. Drake clamped and cut the umbilical cord, she said, "God is great."

I snapped a second picture before another transport nurse left the OR with my new daughter in her arms. The news went out ahead of her, "We have a nice, pink baby girl."

Next up popped Natalie Sue.

Bobbi

As I stared at the surgical drape in front of my face, the anesthesiologist kept up a running commentary. He told me, "She's making the incision now." A moment later he said, "She's moving the bladder flap aside." What a strange sensation to feel all that tugging and pulling on my body, but without any pain!

I had strained to try to see our first baby when Dr. Mahone announced his arrival. Tears came to my eyes when Kenny spoke his name. When Dr. Drake said, "God is great," my tears threatened to overflow. When Alexis was born, I strained my ears in vain for some sound from my baby girl.

Watching the nurses rush Kenneth, and then Alexis, out of the room, I wondered if they really were okay. I heard the comment about Kenneth's size. I knew someone had said that Alexis looked good. But I had no real indication of just how they were doing. I hadn't been able to see them moving. I couldn't even be sure they were breathing.

Until the next baby was born. I heard Dr. Mahone say, "It's another girl."

"Position?" someone asked.

"Transverse," another voice answered.

As soon as she came out, I heard her cry—for only a moment or two. I cried quite a bit longer. *At least one of the babies seems to be okay!* I thought.

Tears continued to stream down my face as I heard Kenny say, "This is Natalie Sue."

I cried even more when I heard Dr. Drake say once again, "God is great!"

Everything seemed to be happening very fast. And it was. Once the doctors interrupted the flow of blood to my uterus, that began to disrupt the flow of blood and oxygen to the babies. Each remaining baby ran an increased risk of losing blood and developing complications. So Dr. Mahone pulled babies out as fast as she could. Kenneth was born at 12:48 P.M., Alexis at 12:49 P.M., and Natalie at 12:50 P.M.

Next came Kelsey Ann at 12:51. Dr. Mahone lifted her out, saying, "Breech." (Meaning she presented buttocks-first.) "It's another girl!"

Kenny named her. From behind a surgical mask, someone said, "Look at those cheeks!" And Dr. Drake said, "God is great!"

"All the rest are boys," Kenny reminded everyone.

Nathan Roy was born at 12:52. Dr. Mahone announced, "It's a boy." Nathan let out a wail as Kenny said his name.

"Wow, listen to that one!" someone exclaimed.

"All right!" another approving voice added.

Dr. Drake repeated, "God is great."

Dr. Mahone brought Brandon James out at 12:53. "It's a boy . . . vertex." (Vertex meant he presented headfirst.)

Kenny introduced him by name. Someone laughed and said, "He certainly doesn't look like a girl!"

And as she clamped and cut his umbilical cord, Dr. Drake said, "God is great!"

"Just one more left to get out," said Dr. Mahone.

That was Joel, born at 12:54 P.M.—the seventh baby born in just over six minutes. Dr. Mahone pulled him out, saying, "It's a boy."

Joel let out a loud, lusty cry. And he kept crying.

Kenny raised his voice a little to be heard over the cries of our youngest son and said, "And this . . . is Joel Steven."

To the tune of Joel's crying, Dr. Drake concluded with, "And God . . . *is* . . . good."

Fifteen

I Want to See My Babies

Bobbi

"Are there any more in there?" asked Kenny.

"No!" answered Dr. Mahone. Everyone in the operating room laughed at Kenny's joke. Then he squeezed my hand and said, "They are all so beautiful! You did a good job."

"Will you be all right, dearie, if I go check on the babies?"

"Go!" I urged him. "Check on our new family!" Kenny kissed me good-bye and I settled back as the doctors delivered the placentas and sewed up my incision. That took several times longer than the babies' births. While the doctors stitched, I dozed off, an aftereffect of the epidural.

Much to my—and the doctors'—relief, my uterus began the normal process of contracting back to its original size. If it hadn't (one of the possible serious complications of a multiple birth) I would have needed an emergency hysterectomy. With seven babies, my uterus had stretched so far, no one could predict what it would do. Thank goodness that extra surgery wasn't necessary!

When Dr. Mahone had finished with the stitches, she told me that she wanted to do an internal exam. In the process, she measured my cervix.

"Your cervix is six centimeters dilated!" she told me. "Have you been having contractions?" (A cervix is fully dilated—and ready for a baby to be born—when it reaches ten centimeters.)

"I've had contractions all morning," I said. "Some of them were strong. But we never timed them to see if they were regular."

"Well, you really were in labor," she concluded. "You don't have to worry about whether or not you did the right thing by going ahead with the birth. It might have been a little later, but we would have had these babies today, anyway."

Then I'm glad we went ahead with a scheduled C-section. That's better than an emergency one! I thought. *Now, let's get this part over with. I want to see my babies!*

Kenny

I knew that our families were anxious for news. Before I headed to the holding room to see the babies, I made a detour into the lounge where they were waiting. I walked through the door and looked at the crowd of people who loved us.

I managed to get out these words, "Four boys, three girls, all healthy," before I began to cry. Amid their joyful exclamations and my tears, I added, "Three of them screamed."

Someone commented, "Must have seen you!" And laughter joined the other happy comments.

"They're pretty big, are they?" my father-in-law asked.

"They're good-sized." I held up my hands like a fisherman bragging on his catch.

Our pastor summed up all our feelings by beginning to sing the Doxology. Few eyes in the room were dry as we all joined him:

Praise God from whom all blessings flow.
Praise Him all creatures here below.
Praise Him above ye heavenly host.
Praise Father, Son, and Holy Ghost. Amen.

Then I accepted a few hugs and headed to the holding room to see our children.

Four or five people hovered over each of the small beds containing our babies. Ohio beds were designed for stabilizing newborn babies, and each one had heat lamps, an oxygen hood, a heart monitor, a temperature sensor, and an Oximeter to measure how well the baby's blood was oxygenating. But the top of each bed was open, allowing the doctors and nurses easy access to the babies.

I went from one baby to the next, speaking to each by name. "Hi there, Natalie. I'm your dad. Your mom and I love you!"

I looked at them in amazement; they were breathing and moving and wonderful. I watched while nurses turned babies over back to front, then front to back. Doctors inserted IVs into arms or umbilical cords. Respiratory therapists hooked each baby up to a ventilator. Dr. Robert Shaw, a neonatologist and the medical director of the neonatal intensive care unit (NICU) at Blank Children's Hospital, moved from one bed to the next, supervising his colleagues.

The atmosphere of the room was busy, urgent, almost frantic, with so many people moving about and with machines beeping or humming. But each member of the medical team went about their business briskly, doing his or her particular role. Everywhere I looked there was a healthy, pink, breathing, moving baby.

As I walked around the room, the doctors and nurses talked to me:

"Congratulations, Mr. McCaughey!"

"She's a big one!"

"He's pink and healthy."

"How beautiful!"

Little Kenneth had begun to cry in the hallway between the OR and the holding room. Neither Bobbi nor I had heard his cries. But the medical personnel in the holding room had heard Kenny coming, and the specialists waiting for him had applauded at the sound.

Hours and hours of preparation had gone into the quiet action I was witnessing in that holding room. The doctors and nurses had tried to prepare themselves for every possible emergency. These specialists had experience treating babies in trouble—babies too small and too blue. They were ready for some serious problems. No one had dared hope that the birth would go so smoothly. The atmosphere was full of joy and electricity: Our babies were plump, pink, and active beyond anyone's expectations.

As each baby was stabilized and ready to head for the NICU, a nurse would pick him up and carry him out into the hallway. She'd place him into a transport isolette, an enclosed, high-tech, rolling bed with portable monitors and ventilation equipment on board. Then a security guard accompanied each baby and three-member medical transport team on a four-minute ride down the hall, into an elevator, and into Blank Children's Hospital, located in an attached building on the Iowa Methodist Medical Center's forty-two-acre campus.

My dad was out in the hallway with his video camera. He had dressed in green scrubs, planning to videotape in the delivery room. But at the last minute, we were informed that he would not be allowed to do that. The hospital public relations people were the only ones permitted to videotape in the OR. So Dad tried to make up for it by videotaping as much as possible in the hallways and in the neonatal nursery.

Once in the NICU, each baby was transferred to another Ohio bed, and a team of NICU nurses took over and began their own admittance examinations. I escorted several of the transport isolettes all the way up to the nursery. There I'd reach through the tubes and wires around the Ohio bed to briefly stroke the arm or leg of my child and speak to him again.

Each time I reentered the OR holding room, it seemed that another one of our children was stable and ready for transport to the nursery. So, I checked on each baby left there before making another four-minute trip beside another transport isolette, down the hall and up the Blank Children's Hospital elevator to the NICU. After the first three or four, I just waited there in the nursery for the others to arrive.

Our friends and family soon made their way to the NICU to see the babies. Hospital security had issued white wristbands to our family members. And only the people with these wristbands were allowed into our section of the NICU.

Not long after Joel arrived, Dr. Holley Bzdega, one of the neonatologists at Blank Children's Hospital, approached me.

"Mr. McCaughey, may I have a word with you?" she asked. Noting the worried frown on her face, I followed her over to Joel's bed.

"Joel is experiencing some difficulty." Those were words I did not want to hear.

"He has lost color," she continued. "We are afraid that he is bleeding internally. He needs a blood transfusion—and he needs it now."

The doctors wanted permission immediately. *Lord, help me make the right decision,* I prayed. Then I said, "Sure, whatever you need to do."

I stood over Joel, as the specialists began replacing his lost blood, and I whispered, "Hi there, Joel. I'm your daddy. I love you. There are a lot of people out here rooting for you. Be a fighter, Joel! Be strong."

I asked Pastor to call the prayer chain and get our church friends praying for Joel. Our family began praying too.

By this time Bobbi had been transferred to a recovery room where I found her and filled her in on what was happening with Joel. She and I together asked God to take care of this precious little one.

We were worried for our child. And I'm glad we didn't know then all that we learned later.

As the last baby born, Joel was at highest risk for internal bleeding. Later the doctors determined he had bled through his placenta during the birth. But at the time, when they noted his loss of color, the doctors worried that he was bleeding internally, in either his brain or his abdomen, a common risk associated with premature babies.

Joel had lost so much blood that he could have experienced renal failure or cardiac arrest. His kidneys should have shut down. Instead, that first day, he had more urine output than any of the other babies. And, within minutes of starting the transfusion and the prayer chain, he pinked right up. And all was well again.

I was still in the recovery room with Bobbi when it was time to watch the press conference where her dad, Bob Hepworth, planned to issue the official birth announcement. We watched it on the small television in the corner of the room. The reception looked a little fuzzy, but that did nothing to disguise the pride in my father-in-law's voice.

Bobbi

We had been asked for a brief statement. We thought we would come up with something written, an announcement that probably would be edited by the newspapers. We had wondered how best to give the glory for this event to God. We expected it might be cut if we were "too Christian." So Dad had composed a two-line statement we hoped would be suitable.

But, just minutes before Dad's statement, Marlys Popma found out the entire press conference would be carried live on television.

"No one will be able to edit the statement. And no station will cut out on you. So you can go for it," she told my dad, once a Baptist pastor. "You can say all you want to about God."

So when the hospital spokespeople introduced him, he walked to the microphone and said:

> Bobbi and Kenny and their families invite you and indeed the world to join us in praise and thanksgiving to God for this marvelous work that He has done. The babies delivered safely. They delivered at 12:48 to 12:54. And as was said, I am probably one of the proudest grandfathers in this country at this moment.
>
> I would ask that all believers across the world join us in praying for Bobbi and the babies, that their health would continue and only improve.

Bobbi is in the recovery room and resting comfortably. I have the weights of the babies for you. They are currently in serious condition.

Kenneth . . . Kenneth Robert, I might say, named after me, Kenneth weighed 3 pounds, 4 ounces. Alexis weighed 2 pounds, 11 ounces; Natalie weighed 2 pounds, 10 ounces; Kelsey was 2 pounds, 5 ounces; Brandon was 3 pounds, 3 ounces; Nathaniel was 2 pounds, 14 ounces; and Joel was 2 pounds, 15 ounces.

And the family indeed wants to thank you for all of your prayers, for your well-wishing throughout the last few months. Thank you very much.

Kenny and I rejoiced to hear that announcement and to see the pride on my father's face. But when I heard Dad say the name, "Nathaniel," I turned to Kenny and said, "I really like Nathan better than Nathaniel." So we made a last-minute name change for our third son. (We also found out later that the hospital's note Dad was reading from had reversed Nathan's and Brandon's weights.)

Only forty-three minutes after Dr. Mahone delivered the first of our babies, all seven were stabilized and in the NICU. Emotionally, I was more than ready to see them. But I wasn't medically ready to go.

Time in that recovery room just dragged on. Nurses kept coming in and pressing on my stomach, to stimulate my uterus to contract. I remembered this from Mikayla's birth. Only after Mikayla, the procedure was merely annoying. Now, I not only had a fifteen-inch incision from the C-section, but I also had a uterus that had been more than a bit overstretched. Each time someone kneaded my abdomen, the pain nearly sent me through the roof.

As my epidural wore off, I received medication for discomfort. That left me feeling groggy and drifting in and out of sleep. But even that wasn't enough to keep me from hurting when they massaged my uterus.

When I floated "in" all I could think was, *I want to see my babies!*

Finally, two and a half hours after the babies were born, I had regained the feeling in my legs and was ready to take the ride up to the NICU. Nurses wheeled my bed down the hall and into the elevator. Kenny walked beside me and we were all escorted by yet another security guard. When we reached the NICU row where our babies were, our families were already gathered by the door, waiting for me.

I could see the Ohio beds, four on one side of an aisle and three on the other. On the walls above each was a letter, A through G. They had lined the babies up in alphabetical order. But the sides of the beds were so high, I couldn't see the babies in them.

"Can I sit up, please?" I asked the nurse. "I can't really see my babies."

"We can raise you a little," she responded. "But, right after a C-section, you cannot sit up completely." And she elevated the head of my bed just enough so that I could peer over the edge of the cribs and see my children through the maze of IVs and ventilators.

They were so pink! And so much bigger than I had expected. *They are beautiful,* I thought. *Look at those chubby little cheeks.* I reached through the wires and tubes and stroked a tiny arm or leg. I spoke to each baby and told each one how much I loved them. When I saw Brandon, I laughed. "Oh, no! He's got Kenny's toes!" Even that first time, I could see how each baby had his or her own look.

Then, only a half hour after arriving, my nurse insisted it was time for me to go. I was in pain and so sleepy from the pain medicine, I could hardly hold my eyes open. My babies were all breathing. We had the four boys and three girls that the doctors had predicted. No surprises. No eighth baby. No real problems. I could finally let myself drift completely off to sleep. I don't really even remember that ride back to IMMC. For security reasons, I was taken back to Labor and Delivery, to the same room in which I had spent the last seven and a half weeks.

Kenny

That afternoon, while Bobbi and I were visiting the NICU, the doctors conducted a press conference about the birth of our babies. Neither of us watched that. But we heard about it later and were given a copy of the video.

After a couple of the hospital honchos made opening remarks, they introduced our two perinatologists. Paula Mahone told reporters:

> I would like you all to know that Dr. Drake and I feel it has been a real privilege to manage Bobbi's pregnancy. We give God the glory and the praise for her pregnancy, the outcome, the babies, and her decision to continue the pregnancy as God gave it to her.
>
> We both love what we do and enjoy taking care of patients that have high-risk problems during their pregnancies. We knew this would be a challenge . . .
>
> I also want to thank the staff here. We've had many hours of meetings to organize and plan her delivery. I think we did a stellar job . . .

This delivery has helped us reexamine what we do for taking care of mothers and babies here . . . This delivery has helped us reach a new level of enthusiasm.

In answer to reporters' questions she said:

We were all very excited as we delivered each baby and saw the size of each and how vigorous they were. We were all very, very happy. She (Bobbi) had no unusual complications. Everything went very well . . . It was wonderful! All the babies came out very vigorous . . . it was calm in the room, very organized . . . It was an environment where everyone felt great about being there and about helping this patient.

And later,

I would consider this a miracle . . . that all the babies are so well grown, so well developed . . . that this patient did not develop preeclampsia or toxemia, that she had no medical conditions. This strikes me as a miracle! . . .

God had blessed this family and this pregnancy. I believe that wholeheartedly. Bobbi's attitude, toward really wanting these babies, being willing to put up with all the discomforts, the inability to care for herself, and be dependent on other people . . . made the difference. That and the prayers.

One reporter asked, "What things were done to help her (Bobbi) get to 30 weeks of pregnancy?" Dr. Drake's first response was: "Prayer!"

We were thrilled to realize that the doctors and the hospital also felt God's presence that day.

Bobbi

During that press conference, Dr. Mahone told the media something that we did not know until much later. She explained that after my delivery, she had examined the placentas closely. Two of our babies had "velamentous insertions," where the umbilical cord is attached to the side rather than the center of the placenta. Dr. Mahone told the press, "In most situations, that results in a low-birth-weight baby or a growth-restricted child. These babies are not growth restricted in any way!"

The miracles just kept piling up!

Kenny

With Bobbi asleep in her hospital room, I headed back to the NICU, where most of our family members were still gathered, admiring the babies. Dr. Shaw came over and told me that Joel's condition had definitely improved, his color was back, and his blood count was headed up. I shared this good news with our families.

Mikayla had spent the day with our friends, Chuck and Linda Moehring. Now, toward evening, they brought Mikayla up to the hospital NICU.

"Mikayla, these are your new brothers and sisters," I told her. I carried her down one row and back up the other, with introductions. "That's Kenny. That's Alexis and that's Natalie. This one is Kelsey and that one is Nathan. That's Brandon and that one is Joel."

Mikayla looked around solemnly. "Baby!" she told me as she pointed at Joel. "Baby! . . . Baby! . . . Baby! . . . Baby!"

I stood in the middle of the cribs, with Mikayla in my arms, while she pointed at each one in turn. "Baby!"

I was still in the NICU with our babies a little later when Lynn Yontz, public relations director for Blank Children's Hospital, approached me. She told me that Governor Branstad had called the hospital to schedule yet another press conference. "He wants to announce plans to give you and Bobbi a new house."

"What?" *Did I hear her right?* "A new house?"

Lynn nodded, a big grin on her face.

"But," I began to protest, "there isn't a place in Carlisle to build a new house. And we don't want to move out of Carlisle! The only available lots in town would be up on a hill. We don't want to live up on a hill."

I could see from the expression on Lynn's face this wasn't the reaction she expected. But after everything that had already happened that day, this news was simply too much for my overloaded mind and heart to absorb. I was too focused on the overwhelming details to even express gratitude for such generosity.

Fortunately, my father was standing close enough to overhear the conversation. Dad stepped over, put a hand on my arm, and reassured me, "We'll work the details out later, Kenny."

He's right. I gave Ms. Yontz my approval for the press conference, and it was also agreed that a number of relatives would represent our family. A little while later I stepped into an NICU waiting area to catch the announcement on television.

The governor stood in front of Bobbi's parents, my parents, and most of our siblings. First he presented a Winnie the Pooh bear for Mikayla and seven official birthday cards from the governor.

He then declared November 19, 1997, "McCaughey Children's Day." In his proclamation, he said:

Whereas, the community of Carlisle and the McCaughey's extended family of church members have provided love, care, and support for this very special family;

And whereas, Bobbi McCaughey has shown tremendous strength and courage throughout her pregnancy;

And whereas, Bobbi and Kenneth McCaughey are living examples of the word of God;

And whereas, the septuplets are true miracles of life and will be celebrated as such throughout the world . . . I urge all Iowans to pray for continued health and vitality for Bobbi McCaughey and her seven very special gifts to this world.

The governor then had our family members step aside, and he brought out representatives of various Iowa companies who would help with the project he was proposing. He said he understood Bobbi and I lived in a small home and would obviously need a lot more room for our family now. Therefore, he said, he'd begun talking to businesses about building and donating to us a house big enough to meet the needs of our new ten-member family.

Suddenly this idea of a new home seemed real. It's a good thing I was already sitting down, because it was still almost too incredible to believe.

When Bobbi roused to semiconsciousness a little while later, I told her what the governor had said.

"You're kidding!"

"No," I assured her. "He indicated he wanted to talk to us in person soon with more specifics, but it sounds like he's saying they will build a house to our specifications."

"Wow!"

Those were my sentiments as well.

Bobbi

I was pretty much out of it all Wednesday evening. When I was awake my thoughts were on our babies. But the governor's promise to build and give us a new house certainly registered. It seemed way too much to fully comprehend, however.

I kept waiting for someone to shake me and tell me the whole day had been a dream. Just as I kept waiting for someone to turn the spotlight off. *Surely, soon, something else will happen in the world and the press will scurry away and our fifteen minutes of fame will be over. Surely, soon, life will go back to normal.*

Evidently that wasn't going to happen anytime soon.

Thursday morning, less than twenty-four hours after the babies' births, in an effort to satisfy the media's curiosity, Kenny gave a press conference at our home church, Missionary Baptist Church in Carlisle. Now fully awake at last, I was anxious to get over to the NICU to see the babies. First I had to wait for a doctor to check me out. Then I stayed in my room so that I could watch Kenny's news conference, carried live on local television and a number of national cable channels.

Marlys Popma, our family spokesperson, welcomed the media before turning the microphone over to Pastor Brown, who opened the press conference by praying:

> Our Father, we thank You for this blessed event . . . We thank You for protecting and keeping these babies safe all these months . . . Father, we thank You for Kenny and Bobbi, that You've given them this great responsibility and pray that You give them wisdom and direction that they might raise these children to bring honor and glory to the Lord Jesus Christ. Amen.

At the close of his prayer, he also said, "The Missionary Baptist Church rejoices . . . but we recognize that the struggle is not over . . . We remain committed to the McCaughey family . . ."

Pastor Brown concluded his remarks with this scripture, 1 Chronicles 16:24–25: "Declare His glory among the nations, His wonders among all peoples. For the LORD is great and greatly to be praised; He is also to be feared above all gods."

Several other people spoke at the press conference. Dwight Loomis, chairman of the church's McCaughey Committee, talked about the committee's past and continuing commitment to provide housecleaning, laundry, and baby-sitting help.

Kenny's boss, David Wright, of Wright Chevrolet, announced that Chevrolet was giving us a fifteen-passenger 1998 Chevrolet Express Van. He also promised to make a financial donation of $100 for each new or used car sold for the rest of the month.

A city official welcomed our babies to Carlisle. Two local bankers (one of them our good friend Chuck Moehring) announced the opening of bank accounts for our family, and gave addresses to which people could send contributions. HyVee Foods announced that they were giving us a year's worth of groceries.

Then, it was Kenny's turn. "Wow!" he started, with camera lights flashing. "I'd like to welcome you to the Lord's house . . . This is one of the most blessed events that I've ever encountered! . . . We're just ecstatic! . . . Bobbi is doing well . . . We are trusting God to provide."

When a reporter asked Kenny about his hopes and fears, he said, "Our big fear is that this not turn into a big show. This is my family. That is what I want it to be . . . We are not on display."

He went on to say, "God could have given us one. God is

entitled to give us seven. It is my commission as a father to raise them . . . in a normal Christian home."

One reporter commented, "It sounds like you're in an incredible church. Tell us about it." Kenny responded, "We've had a lot of church support in financial, spiritual, and physical ways . . . God's going to use this church and this town to do a wonderful work. And He has been."

At that point, Marlys escorted Kenny away from the microphone.

I was amazed; my husband had seemed so poised! I was also pleased; with his news conference over, I could finally go to see my babies.

Kenny

I was back at the hospital Thursday afternoon with Bobbi when the phone rang and someone said, "Mr. McCaughey, you have a phone call from the President of the United States."

Sixteen

The World Watches

Kenny

My first thought was, *This must be a joke.* But then I heard that distinctive voice say, "Ken! Congratulations!" I didn't have time to think.

"Hello, President, uh . . . Mr. President. How are you doing?"

"Well," he replied. "How are you doing?"

"Oh, I'm a little nervous. I can't believe you called me."

"Has the reality sunk in on you yet?"

"Oh, yeah!"

"Seven pairs of shoes."

"Yes," I said.

"Forty-four thousand diapers."

I didn't know what to say to that. "It's an honor to hear from you, sir," I told him.

"Oh, thanks," he replied. "Well, I've just been thinking about you today. The whole country has been following this, and I just want to wish you well. You are going to be the most watched parents in America for the next eighteen years."

"Oh, boy!" I responded—at the same time thinking, *I hope not!*

"I applaud you and your wife," President Clinton continued. "And how's she doing?"

"Good. She's right here if you want to talk to her."

"Sure," the president responded.

"Okay, Mr. President. Just one moment."

Bobbi, who'd been enjoying watching and listening to me talk to the President of the United States, didn't seem too anxious to talk to him herself. When I handed her the phone she acted as though she'd rather hand it right back. But she put the receiver to her ear and softly said, "Hello."

"Hi! How are you?" the president asked.

"Not too bad," Bobbi told him. "A lot better now than yesterday."

"You sound good. You sound strong."

"Well," Bobbi replied, "I've had good care and good doctors. So I guess they just kept me going."

The president said, "Well, it's just amazing. Everybody up here at the White House has been sitting here wide-mouthed. All of us who raised one, or two kids or three are just amazed. But I admire you, and I think it's great, and I hope it will be a great adventure for you the whole way through."

"Oh, I'm very excited," Bobbi said.

"You know," the president continued, "when those kids all go off to school you will be able to get a job running any major corporation in America. You will be the best-organized manager in the United States."

Bobbi laughed. "That or I'll be in a straitjacket somewhere."

"I doubt that," the president said. "Well, congratulations. I'll let you get back to your family. I just wanted to wish you well. I have been so happy about this. All of us have just been grateful that it came out all right. It's an exciting thing for the whole country."

"Thank you for calling," Bobbi said. Then she handed the phone back to me.

"Hello," I said again.

"I just wanted to say good-bye," President Clinton said to me.

"Okay, Mr. President. And you are more than welcome to come see them if you'd like."

"I would love to do that. I wish you would bring them here."

I admitted, "That would be nice too."

". . . We'll take their picture sitting behind the desk in the Oval Office and they can fight about which one of them gets to be president. How's that?"

"That'll work!" I chuckled.

"All right, man."

"Okay, Mr. President. Thank you for calling." We said good-bye and hung up. Then I looked at Bobbi and we grinned at each other. *The President of the United States called us. Unbelievable!*

Bobbi

For months people had been telling us that having septuplets would be a big news event. We knew our story would make headlines in Iowa, of course. We just couldn't imagine the birth of our children would get much attention in the national news.

So the president's call was one of many surprising indications of the incredibly widespread interest in our babies those first couple of days. Oprah called the hospital. We also received personal congratulations from Peter Jennings at ABC News. Dan Rather sent a fruit basket nearly big enough to feed the entire hospital. At one point Marlys Popma had Connie Chung on hold while she talked with another national news figure about our story.

A few days before the babies' births, Marlys had presented to us a fifteen-page list of interview requests. Now it seemed everyone else and his brother wanted desperately to get his foot in our door. David Letterman sent his congratulations and *Late Show* ball caps for everyone in the family. Jay Leno enclosed *Tonight Show* T-shirts along with his good wishes.

We found out later we had the "honor" of being monologue subject matter on both of their shows. Letterman did a "Top Ten List" on the neatest things about having septuplets. Leno cracked a line about child-rearing books. He referred to First Lady Hillary Clinton's book, titled *It Takes a Village,* and suggested, "Bobbi McCaughey's book could be *I Had a Village.*" I got a good laugh when I heard that.

Not only had the births of our babies led every network's evening newscast on Wednesday, updates on the babies continued to be a top story on every morning and prime-time news show for the next few days. When I woke up in the mornings I could have checked on the condition of the babies simply by turning on the television to any number of stations and watching the live, on-camera briefings being given to the media by IMMC's director of the NICU.

Our own folks, proud grandparents that they were, didn't have to content themselves with simply telling their friends and neighbors about the latest additions to their extended family. They got to brag on their grandbabies to people like NBC's Katie

Couric and on shows like ABC's *Good Morning America* as the entire country listened in.

Local newspapers even carried an interview with my twelve-year-old brother, Dennis, whose picture appeared under the headline: "Babies' uncle offers them his wisdom." Describing his first visits with me after the babies were born, Dennis told reporters, "I just looked at her and said, 'Wow!' First she was like a balloon, now she'd popped."

Yet despite the astounding amount of worldwide attention our story received, Kenny and I remained oblivious to most of it those first couple of days. Marlys continued to screen all interview requests for family members and the hospital beefed up the security in the hallway outside my room.

Everyone wanted to give me time to recover my strength and allow Kenny and me to concentrate our attention and energies on our family. The strategy seemed to be working. The babies and I had a much better second night.

Kenny

Friday morning Marlys came to Bobbi's hospital room to talk to both of us. She told us the media wanted to see and hear Bobbi and she thought we needed to decide what to do about all the interview requests.

We both wished the press would just disappear. But they obviously weren't going anywhere until they heard from the mother of the septuplets. Bobbi reluctantly agreed to do one interview later that morning with Molly Cooney from KCCI, the local CBS affiliate. We felt that we owed Molly the first interview since she had honored our wishes and agreed not to break the story when Bobbi had entered the hospital in early October.

We did the interview together, sitting side by side on the bed as Marlys, Molly, and the TV cameraman crowded into Bobbi's hospital room. I think Bobbi said a little more than I did in what turned out to be a fifteen-minute interview.

When pressed to discuss her personal reaction to our amazing experience, Bobbi tried to downplay her private feelings. "I know it's extraordinary or whatever to have this many babies and go this far," she admitted. "But it's something I just did. They were my children and I wanted them."

Asked about our decision not to opt for aborting some babies through selective reduction in order to improve the survival chances of the others, Bobbi told Molly Cooney, "They were all babies and I was going to have them all. How can you decide that you're going to have this one and you're not going to have that one?"

We also told Molly we'd been watching and reading the interviews with friends and neighbors in Carlisle. We'd been particularly amused by the frequent question, "How did you keep it a secret?"

Bobbi said, "We never asked anybody to keep it a secret. They just did. Everybody knew. We would tell people. The people here at the hospital knew. And nobody just ever said anything."

KCCI aired the interview on their noon news that day, advertising it as a "World Exclusive." They shared it with the CBS network, which was to be expected. But when they also released the tape to CNN, the media pool at the hospital went ballistic.

Marlys weathered the initial blast and then came to us. "Everyone's been waiting patiently up till now," she said. "But now that CBS and CNN have your interview with Molly, everyone else is feeling slighted. And they're getting angry about it. We've got to give them something. And soon. All the coverage has been wonderfully positive so far, but I'm afraid that's about to change. The people who don't have anything new to report are upset; if we don't act fast they are going to turn on you. And they are going to turn on me first. Last time I saw them I felt as if they were ready to tear me apart."

We trusted Marlys. But we didn't know what to do.

"They haven't seen Bobbi yet," Marlys pressed. "I think we need to go down and announce that we'll have a press conference with both of you there this afternoon."

Her suggestion made sense to me. After my experience with the press conference at our church the day before, I'd come to view the press as something like a pack of hungry, barking dogs. If we could throw them a bone or two they'd pounce on that and give us a little peace. But until we gave them something new to gnaw on, they were going to keep right on hounding us.

"Let's set it up," I told Marlys. "I think we need to do it."

Bobbi wasn't so sure. "I don't want to do a news conference," she told us. "I just don't think I can."

It took Marlys and me together to finally persuade her that she didn't really have a choice. In the end I think Bobbi conceded mostly because she didn't want to make things any more unpleasant for Marlys in dealing with the press.

No sooner did Marlys announce the hastily planned news conference than the small hospital auditorium began to fill with television cameras, lights, photographers, and reporters. The crush of camera people at the front of the auditorium got so wild Marlys almost called the whole thing off while we were waiting in a back hall for our cue to come out on the stage.

"You're not going to let them mob Bobbi like that, are you?" some reporter asked. "Someone is going to get hurt!"

Marlys agreed and called for more hospital security to intervene. The security people took one look at the mob of reporters and suggested Marlys might have more luck controlling the crowd than they would. Taking charge of the situation, she walked out to the microphone and announced that Bobbi would not appear as long as photographers crowded the stage. "Everyone needs to back up at least a couple of steps."

Surprisingly, the media complied without any protest. A line was taped on the floor and Marlys warned everyone in the room that she would end the press conference immediately if anyone crossed that line.

Bobbi

While all this commotion went on inside the auditorium, I sat, attached to an IV stand, in a wheelchair parked in a back hallway. "I don't want to go in there!" I told Kenny between sobs. "I just can't!"

I didn't think Kenny was being very sympathetic at all. "You can do this," he insisted. "I know you can. You heard Marlys. You *have* to do this!"

I kept crying.

Pastor Brown walked up about that time and was alarmed to see my reaction. He'd never seen me cry before; but then, I hardly ever let anyone see me cry. "You know you don't have to do this press conference if you don't want to," Pastor assured me.

"But Kenny says I have to," I managed to blubber.

Next thing I knew Marlys was telling us it was time to go in. I wanted to hide. But Kenny kept saying, "You can do this!" So I stood up, and as watching security guards surrounded us, I took my husband's arm and went through that door feeling much like the early Christians must have felt walking into the Forum to face the lions.

The next day's *Des Moines Register* reported the scene this way: "Wearing a royal blue robe with gold piping, she stepped onto a small auditorium stage at Iowa Methodist Medical Center. As cameras clicked, she stopped and flinched, appearing frightened."

I think the reporter was being kind—first describing my decidedly unglamorous attire as if I were part of some fashion show, then saying I "stopped" (*froze* was more like it), "appearing frightened." I'm sure I looked every bit as *petrified* as a deer caught in the headlights of an 18-wheeler doing 70 on the interstate at three o'clock in the morning.

If Kenny hadn't taken my arm and gently guided me to a seat behind a table there on that stage, I might still be standing there, tethered to my IV stand like a strange statue on a leash.

I don't remember much from that press conference. I could see little more than the outline of the people crowding the room behind the glare of the TV lights and the almost continuous explosion of camera flashes. And I spoke only reluctantly—using very few words. At the outset I wasn't sure I could manage any words at all.

Looking out at all those camera lenses aimed right at me, I started to speak and the words stuck in my throat. "I can't!" I whispered to Kenny.

He held my hand and said, "I guess I'll talk for Bobbi. This is really overwhelming for her. This is the first time she's had dealings with the media."

As if he were an old pro at it!

Kenny went on to say we wanted to let the world know what had happened. He acknowledged what was obvious, that we weren't quite used to this kind of attention. At least not "Here in little old Iowa—where the tall corn grows . . . and the babies do too."

The entire auditorium erupted with laughter. Noting a smile on my face, Kenny asked if there was anything I wanted to say. I took another stab at it:

"Thank you for the way this has all been handled . . ." Choking up once again, I went on. "When we said, 'Please wait,' you did." So much for not ever letting anyone see me cry; the whole world seemed to be there with cameras recording every tear.

Kenny announced that I would take a couple of questions. NBC's Ann Curry asked what it had been like to actually hold the first of our seven babies that morning.

I did manage a slight smile at the wonderful memory. "It was so unexpected," I said. "I never thought any of them would come off the ventilators this quickly. It was just incredible . . . I can't wait till I can hold them all . . ." My emotions overwhelmed me again.

"If we have the arms for it," Kenny pitched in, stretching one arm out as if for a measurement. The crowd of reporters all laughed.

I turned and looked at my husband in disbelief. Here I was breaking into tears again, and he'd become a wisecracking comedian. Compared to me, he really was an old pro. He clearly took to the limelight faster than I did.

Someone asked me to describe just how I'd held little Kenny. I explained that I cradled him in my arms as you would any small baby, but I had to do so carefully because, despite being off the ventilator, he was still attached to numerous tubes and monitor wires.

At that point Kenny's dad came out on the stage to escort me back to my room. And I gladly left center stage to my husband, who just as happily volunteered to stay and answer more questions.

I learned later that the reporters also asked him to tell about holding Kenny. They asked whether we realized what we were in for, raising so many babies, and how we thought we could manage it. Kenny said we had both learned how to budget our time and planned "to do a lot of things in a limited amount of time." He admitted we'd learned a few things through the years about pinching pennies and we'd been planning all along to make do on our own limited resources. But he admitted to being overwhelmed at the generosity of so many people that God was using to provide for our needs. When the media wanted to know when they would get their first look at the babies and whether or not we'd be selling photos or signing to do a movie of the week, Kenny told them it was far too early for us to have even thought about some of those things. There were so many decisions to make that our answer to most of the remaining questions was "We just don't know yet."

Kenny

That Friday afternoon press conference wasn't our last dealing with the media that day. Marlys informed us that both *Time* and *Newsweek* wanted cover photos of us. "No interviews, just the photos. They need them tonight. So we'd have to shoot them here in your room—one right after the other."

Bobbi told her we wanted to spend time in the nursery with the babies. Marlys promised to tell them it had to be quick. So we agreed.

We also committed to giving NBC's *Dateline* first crack at telling our story and showing our babies to a nationwide audience. We made that decision for several reasons. First, because we often watch the show. Second, we continued to hope that once the story went national and the public was introduced to the babies, the spotlight would go off and we could get on with living our lives. And third, Ann Curry, the *Today Show* anchor who'd flown to Des Moines from New York the day before to make a personal pitch to do a *Dateline* piece, had impressed us as well as our friends and family.

After the news conference at the church on Thursday, Ann had introduced herself to Pastor Brown, who then introduced her to my dad and Val. Ann told them that she had high-risk pregnancies with her five-year-old daughter and two-year-old son. "I want to get the story because I know I would do it justice," she said.

We had more requests and offers than we would ever have time to consider. It seemed more people contacted Marlys's office every hour saying they wanted to do the story. Some, unlike the major networks such as NBC, even offered money. One weekly tabloid started the bidding at $20,000 and kept increasing their offer for exclusive photos and a story until they reached half a million dollars. When we still declined, saying we didn't think their publication was compatible with our personal spiritual values as Christians, they began citing all the articles they'd done about Christian leaders such as Billy Graham and James Dobson and talked about how many Christian readers they had. If that wasn't enough to convince us, they also upped the ante by implying they were willing to do whatever it took for the story.

We soon discovered that for tabloids "whatever it took" not only meant money, it meant tactics.

Seventeen

In the Public Eye

Kenny

We learned from the IMMC security people that one tabloid offered a hospital parking valet $300,000 if he would sneak into the neonatal unit and get them the first published pictures of our babies. (He declined their offer.) A couple of tabloid reporters even knocked at the door of our house and told Bobbi's sister Michele they were delivering flowers. Only after she let them in did they tell her who they really were. She ordered them out immediately, but before they left they took a quick look around. Other representatives of the same publication offered one of our family members several thousand dollars just for a wedding photo of Bobbi and me; that offer also was turned down.

It would take weeks before we learned they would never take no for an answer. But that Friday night we naively hoped, when they learned our standards weren't any more for sale than our babies were, the tabloids would just give up and leave us alone.

Bobbi

Friday had turned out to be quite an emotional day for every-one. The decision made to interview with Ann Curry on Monday afternoon, we still had the *Newsweek* and *Time* cover shots to do.

The *Newsweek* photographer set up in one room. We did that shot with me wearing my glamorous blue bathrobe (the one trimmed with gold piping). Then, at Marlys's suggestion, and to both photographers' relief, I slipped on a red robe (in keeping with *Time's* traditional cover color) and walked across the hall with Kenny to have another cover photo taken.

By the time we finished that ordeal we'd all had our fill of media attention. Marlys announced that she was quitting her job as family spokesperson—for the rest of the day. She risked being mobbed if she tried walking around the hospital without a per-sonal security escort. She promised to be back in the morning but said she was turning off her two cellular phones and going home for the night.

Kenny and I made an escape of our own—to the neonatal inten-sive care unit where we stayed with our babies until bedtime. There in the welcome quiet of the NICU, moving from one Ohio bed to the next, stroking tiny arms and legs and whispering our love to Kenny, Natalie, Alexis, Kelsey, Brandon, Nathan, and Joel, the rest of the world ceased to exist.

Kenny

There were no press conferences scheduled for Saturday. The hospital went so far as to announce they would not even give medical updates on Bobbi or the babies over the weekend. That meant a number of the satellite trucks pulled out. It also meant we didn't have to deal with the media—except for Ann Curry and her *Dateline* producer, Jamie Bright, who arrived to conduct a preinterview for their special.

When Curry and Bright first showed up at the labor and delivery unit to talk to us, hospital security refused to let them in. When I heard the commotion down the hall I went to see if I could help. I found a standoff taking place between the NBC team and an unbudging guard.

I quickly explained to our sentry that we'd given our permission for an interview and were expecting these folks. The man responded politely but firmly, telling me that might well be, but he had his orders, which he had to abide by until officially instructed otherwise. And those orders were that no unauthorized people were allowed onto this ward.

It took a while to get the guard's instructions altered; all the official order changers seemed to be gone for the weekend. Eventually, we did get the necessary clearance for NBC to come in.

As aggravating as security was for our visitors, we remained thankful for such a wary presence. Not only did the guards guarantee our privacy by keeping out unwelcome media, they also provided a reassuring sense of protection.

For among the piles of correspondence we'd already received from well-wishers were a few crackpot threats and angry tirades from obviously disturbed individuals who'd been set off by the extensive media coverage our family had received. Some merely questioned the validity of fertility treatments in an "already overpopulated world" and complained about our publicly giving God the credit for a "miracle" when our seven babies were "obviously the result of science."

But there were other, truly ugly letters condemning us and our family and wishing harm on the babies. We saw one especially hateful, profanity-laced letter from a person so disturbed he'd written to urge the nurses in the NICU to "kill the seven little rats." So we didn't mind the "inconvenience" of conscientious security guards stationed down the hall from Bobbi's room and outside the doors of the NICU.

However, Saturday turned out to be the best day yet. The doctors had warned Bobbi that after so many months confined to bed she would probably need physical therapy before she would be strong enough to walk again. They once again underestimated my wife. Bobbi felt so much better that we spent most of the remaining hours of Saturday over in the NICU with our babies and with the steady stream of family members who came to see them. In fact she felt strong enough to walk from her room to the hospital cafeteria for supper.

Bobbi

The security system that helped keep the media out of our faces couldn't keep our faces out of the media. The continued interest in our story both amazed and concerned us. We lost track of how many times our parents and other family members were interviewed for weekend news programs. Two large photos of Kenny and me at our Friday afternoon press conference appeared on the front page of Saturday's *Des Moines Register*. Inside the paper were several related stories about: Kenny coming off the ventilator; how the septuplets' births had put Iowa on the healthcare map; a column in tribute to our perinatologists Dr. Mahone and Dr. Drake; child-rearing advice to us from the newspaper's readers; and a complete transcript of our phone conversation on Thursday with President Clinton.

There seemed to be no end to the interest in our story or the angles reporters tried to take to produce copy. Saturday's paper even carried an article telling how Molly Cooney had managed her "exclusive" interview the day before. It included sour-grapes quotes from competing TV stations in the Des Moines market actually questioning the ethics and journalistic integrity of Molly and KCCI for respecting our wishes and holding the story.

The most unbelievable (and kind of funny) news in Saturday's paper appeared in a small box accompanying the front-page story. The sidebar said:

> The excitement over the McCaughey septuplets has reached as far as Alberta, Canada, where leaders of Bobbi McCaughey's hometown are considering renaming a street in her honor.
>
> . . . After news about the septuplets reached the town, there was even talk of turning her former home into a museum. But the talk will remain just that, because it turns out the building was torn down years ago . . .

I wanted to laugh at the absurdity of this sudden celebrity. *Before we had septuplets we were just Kenny and Bobbi. Except for our families and a few friends no one in the world knew or cared what happened to us. Now everyone wants a piece of us. The "hometown" I haven't lived in since infancy suddenly wants to name a street after me. It's all so crazy!*

We're "important" now because of what happened Wednesday afternoon. And yet we are the same people we were on Tuesday. We haven't changed. The only thing that has changed is other people's perception of us. We are now celebri-ties simply because we had seven babies in one day.

The more I thought about it, the less I felt like laughing and the more I wanted to cry. In fact, I did cry as I talked to my parents about all the overwhelming things that were happening. On the one hand I recognized and appreciated the incredible experience we were having, but in tears I told them, "We didn't ask for all this attention, we don't deserve all the things people are giving us. There are so many other people who have just as many needs as we do and no one gives them diapers and formula and new cars and bigger houses.

"I don't want friends or family members feeling we're some-how different or better than they are now because of all this." Not only was I determined that this experience not change who we are, I was even more concerned that it not change our rela-tionships—especially those relationships with the people clos-est to us. Our neighbors, our church friends, and especially our families.

Speaking of families, the nicest surprise of that Saturday was the unexpected arrival of my uncle Henry Hepworth, Dad's brother, from Three Hills, Alberta. Since I hadn't seen Uncle Henry for eight years, I determined before I went to bed that night that I'd check out of the hospital the next morning so I could go home to Carlisle and spend a little more time with Uncle Henry before he had to head back to Canada on Monday.

When I declared my intentions to the doctors, they told me they saw no reason I had to stay. The decision was up to me.

As I tried to fall asleep that evening I kept thinking, *Tomorrow I finally get to go home to Kenny and Mikayla.* Exciting as that prospect was, I also kept wondering, *How am I going to go home and leave my babies here in the hospital?*

Kenny

Since I planned to check Bobbi out of the hospital by nine or ten o'clock Sunday morning, I didn't make it to church with the rest of the family. I learned later I missed a very special service.

So many reporters and television cameras lined up outside and inside the sanctuary that Pastor Brown handed out specially prepared flyers welcoming the media, but spelling out guidelines that would allow them to observe, record, and participate in the service without disrupting or dishonoring the spirit of worship. The ushers had been briefed and were prepared to act as Baptist bouncers if the need arose to escort uncooperative media folks out of the sanctuary. But everyone remained on their best behavior.

Pastor Brown greeted the congregation by saying, "What a great week this has been, hasn't it, in so many ways." He acknowledged the range of emotions so many had felt, "from cautious anticipation to glorious exuberance, from physical weariness to having our adrenaline charged."

As one reporter attending the service wrote in his article to appear in the following day's paper,

> Religious leaders could not have asked for a better public relations campaign on the power of faith. Doctors, family members, the community, even the governor have spoken often of God as the story of the McCaughey births unfolded.

"It's almost like letting God out of the closet," a stranger wrote in a letter Pastor Brown read to the congregation.

At the end of the morning service the congregation all stood and sang "To God Be the Glory, Great Things He Hath Done." I wished I could have been there to sing with them.

Our home church in little Carlisle, Iowa, wasn't the only place God was given credit that morning. Bobbi's father was one of a panel of guests to appear on *Face the Nation*. Bob Hepworth reported to viewers on the good health and steady improvement of Bobbi and the babies. He also told the world that our family was ready for the "awesome responsibility" it had been handed. "And we certainly want to thank the country for the interest they've taken," he added. "It is nothing but a miracle of God!"

Bobbi

At the hospital that morning Kenny and I were having our own experience with the media, which proved to be more frustrating than fun or inspiring.

Dateline wanted footage of us with the babies in the nursery before I went home. "It will only take us forty-five minutes," they told us.

Everyone was very nice—especially Ann Curry and her producer, Jamie Bright. They all wanted to be considerate of us and our desire to get home. But that didn't prevent the outcome: It was nearly noon and we were almost three hours behind schedule by the time the cameramen decided they had enough footage.

We found out later that they flew that tape of our babies back to New York strapped to a special courier under his clothes. At the time, we were a lot more concerned about sneaking me out of the hospital without alerting the press than we were about the safe delivery of that first exclusive videotape of our babies to the *Dateline* editors in New York.

The first exit door we tried had reporters outside it. So Kenny and an accompanying security guard reversed course and pushed my wheelchair through the corridors to another door. Reporters were there as well.

No one had been expecting me to go home Sunday. In fact the only word the hospital had given about my release was that I expected to be home before Thanksgiving, which was the coming Thursday. However, in his *Face the Nation* appearance that morning, Dad had let it slip I was headed home today.

By the time we tried the third and fourth exits, another forty-five minutes had passed, and I could tell Kenny was getting frustrated. I knew he just wanted to let me go home in privacy and not have to face the cameras again. But I didn't want him to be upset.

"It's okay!" I assured him.

Kenny

No, it wasn't okay. All I wanted to do was take my wife home from the hospital without making a public spectacle of her. As usual, the media had us completely surrounded.

"I've got an idea," our security escort told me. He pulled out his walkie-talkie and instructed someone on the other end to go out to the employee parking lot and pull his pickup into a closed courtyard at the center of the hospital. "There won't be any cameras in there," he said.

I gave our car keys to my dad and Val who'd arrived at the hospital early enough to see some of the *Dateline* taping. "Meet us at the A&W Drive-In over in Indianola," I told them. "Bobbi says she's hungry and we can eat in the car without being recognized there."

Then Bobbi and I went with our escort to the courtyard where all three of us crowded into the cab of his S-10 pickup. Bobbi and

I slumped down as he smuggled us out of the hospital past the reporters and satellite trucks still filing their story updates with their studios around the country.

We had no trouble rendezvousing at our favorite root beer stand. No one seemed to recognize us when we placed our order. Nevertheless, by the time we drove into Carlisle, news vans and satellite trucks lined the street in front of our house.

One of the private security guards *Dateline* had hired to provide twenty-four-hour protection held the cameras at bay when I pulled into our driveway. A second guard opened the gate so I could pull around back and out of sight. "We caught a couple of tabloid photographers climbing over your back fence a while ago," he told us as I hurried Bobbi through the back door of the house. "But it's all clear now."

Nearly eight weeks after Bobbi had left to go into the hospital, we were finally home. She sagged to the couch in exhaustion.

The first thing I did was walk around to every window in the house to close the blinds. I wondered if the day would ever come again when I wouldn't feel like a prisoner in my own home.

Eighteen

Divided Hearts

Bobbi

Because of the loss of muscle mass resulting from months of bed rest, I had gained only twenty-eight pounds during my pregnancy. Then I dropped fifty pounds when the babies were born.

I loved my new skinny feeling. But when I went to my closet to get dressed for church that first Sunday night, nothing fit.

"I'm going to have to go shopping," I told Kenny. "None of my clothes fit."

The next day, Kenny and I saw the babies at the hospital in the morning. We interviewed on-camera for *Dateline* in the afternoon. That evening we took Mikayla and went out to eat at one of our favorite restaurants and then Kenny took me shopping.

"Just get whatever you want," Kenny told me. He didn't even suggest a price limit, something that had never happened before. I could have broken the bank. Instead I spent a hundred dollars on new clothes.

Being home again was wonderful. Oh, how I had missed Mikayla! Before I had gone to the hospital, our little girl had been at the center of my world. Kenny and I rarely went anywhere without her.

So I loved getting her back. Heaven couldn't be much better than how it felt to get up in my own house those first few mornings. I'd wait for Mikayla to wake up and come stumbling sleepy-eyed out of her room to find me, climb into my arms, and exclaim, "Hi, Mommy! I love you!" Nothing else in the world warms my heart or starts my day better than that.

What luxury to sleep in the soothing warmth of my own waterbed, after so many weeks of discomfort in my cold, hard, and lonely hospital bed. How I had missed sleeping next to my husband. Yes, it felt fantastic to be home! To be a family again.

But *home* is more than a cozy house with friendly walls and familiar surroundings. Home truly is where the heart is! And a huge part of my heart remained in that neonatal intensive care unit of Blank Children's Hospital more than a dozen miles away.

Until all seven of our babies could join the rest of us in Carlisle, I realized my mother's heart would be divided. I knew that until we—all ten of us—were finally under one roof together, I could never again feel I was totally, truly *home*.

For so many months all our hopes and prayers and impatience had been focused on keeping our seven babies healthy and having them here. Now that they'd finally arrived *here* in the world so safely, so surprisingly strong, our entire focus shifted to getting them healthy enough to have them *here*, with us as a real family, in our own house on First Avenue in Carlisle.

We went to the hospital at least once, often twice, every day. Kenny didn't have to go back to work until Friday, the day after

Thanksgiving. So the two of us spent as much time as we could with the babies that week.

The *Dateline* show we had taped with Ann Curry on Sunday and Monday aired nationwide on NBC Tuesday evening, just seven days after the births. Jamie Bright, the *Dateline* producer, stayed in Des Moines so she could join us and our families in Mom and Dad's basement when we gathered to watch the broadcast together.

Watching the video of our babies on the screen I couldn't help thinking: *Most parents of newborns shoot a fast roll of poorly exposed snapshots they can proudly show off to friends and send to more distant relatives. Our kids get live, special-bulletin, breaking-news birth announcements courtesy of Dan Rather, Tom Brokaw, and Peter Jennings. And less than a week later their first pictures are broadcast on nationwide television in a "news special" hyped by the network and seen by millions.*

What a strange mixture of feelings I had sitting and watching my family's life played out live and in color on NBC television. I reacted with the usual maternal pride as everyone in the family "oohed and aaahed" over my children's pictures.

But watching myself on screen was a less-than-pleasant experience. I'd felt tongue-tied and nervous enough when we'd taped the interviews. Watching it all replayed in front of my eyes made me feel even more uncomfortable. No matter how many friends and relatives told me, "You did great!" I couldn't believe them. The Bobbi McCaughey I saw on television always seemed so uneasy, so inarticulate that I thought it painfully obvious I was completely out of my element in front of a camera.

By the time the credits rolled at the end of the show, I was thinking, *I never want to go through something like that again.* As far as I was concerned, the best thing about the broadcast was that it was over with.

My goal, which I'd guarded in the back of my mind for weeks, had been to be home by Thanksgiving. I'd told Molly Cooney, in that first television interview in my hospital room, that I planned to be home by Thanksgiving, "even if I have to walk home!"

So when our family gathered for a traditional Thanksgiving feast at Ken and Val's house that Thursday, my heart was already more full than my stomach could ever be (or had been a few days earlier). As Kenny's dad said the blessing for the meal, he also thanked God for the babies' safety and the miracle of their births. Once again, I cried.

Never in my life had I imagined so much for which to be thankful.

After we devoured all the turkey and dressing and potatoes and cranberry sauce and pumpkin pie we could manage, Mikayla stayed with her grandfather, while Kenny and I, along with Val and her mother, Doris Templeton, headed for the hospital. There we spent the remainder of the holiday with the rest of our family.

Kenny

As we ate our Thanksgiving dinner at Dad and Val's house, I heard a car driving very slowly down the street in front of their house. I walked to the front window and watched it cruise by. A few minutes later, through the rumble of the conversation, I heard the sound of that same car pass by again. The third time the car approached the house, I heard the engine shut off. I went to the window again and saw it parked, less than a block away, facing Dad and Val's house.

Oh, no, I thought, *that has to be some crazy reporter! They found out where Dad and Val live. Who knows what they have on their minds?*

222

After a few minutes of watching the car from the safety of the house, wondering what was going on, I decided to check it out. Donning a heavy coat I marched right out the front door and strode briskly toward the lurking vehicle.

Even before I reached the vehicle I realized it was empty. There was no photographer with a telephoto lens; there was no one there at all. Just an empty car, parked on the street. *Probably just someone visiting friends for the holiday and not knowing exactly where their friends lived.*

I felt foolish for having been so suspicious. At the same time, I realized just how much being in the spotlight weighed on my mind.

Bobbi

After the holiday, I went to the hospital every day. Most evenings, when Kenny got off work, we both drove back in to see the babies. Sometimes, if we didn't plan to stay very long, we would take Mikayla with us. The nurses and hospital staff did their best to entertain her. But an active two-year-old will watch babies only so long, particularly babies she can't play or interact with. So, more often than not, Mikayla stayed with grandparents while we made the daily treks to IMMC.

Our church continued to provide meals three nights a week. On those nights, we'd eat as a family at home before driving in. Other nights I would cook supper, or we'd grab drive-in burgers on our way into Des Moines.

Kenny

I can't adequately describe how much I loved going to see the babies. Our hospital pilgrimage became very familiar, but never got old—because every day brought something new. The babies seemed to grow and develop in leaps and bounds.

As we'd get off the elevator near the NICU each night, the security guard would greet us, "Hello, folks! How's everyone doing today?"

"We're about to find out," I'd answer with a smile. We'd wash our hands with red disinfectant soap. Then we'd be ready to see our children.

I always started with little Kenny, in the first crib. I'd walk around the room and speak to each baby, reaching in and touching the tiny bodies as I spoke. Then we would hold and rock any baby who was awake and ready. My goal was to hold all the babies at least five minutes each night. Sometimes the nurses would be too busy with one of them, or they would be asleep. We knew that they needed their sleep, and the nurses' care. But they also needed Mom and Dad.

All our babies were off their ventilators by the end of the first week. They remained attached to various monitor wires and IVs, though, since they were too young to eat on their own. We learned how to avoid tangling all those lines while we held and rocked them in the rocking chairs available in the NICU.

Sometimes I would look at other babies in the unit. One very tiny baby was in a special bubble—a glass dome over his head. Another baby slept in an isolation room near our babies—his lungs wracked by disease. We talked to the parents of those babies, daily asking how their children were doing, just as they would ask about ours.

I'd see such obviously sick babies in the NICU. Then I'd look at ours, pink, healthy, and growing, and I'd feel very grateful for the miracle God had given us.

In early December, Marlys Popma had a talk with us.

"I've taken you as far as I can," she said. "I know how to handle media. But I don't know about arranging book deals, bank accounts, contracts, and such. You need an agent. And I need to get back to my work."

We appreciated all Marlys Popma did for us. We were grateful to the Iowa Family Policy Center for allowing her to donate nearly six weeks of her time to being our family spokesperson. She had truly been a gift from God. And she was now a dear friend.

God had clearly provided everything we had needed so far. Just as clearly, we knew we wanted to spend our time and energy on our family, not on sorting out stacks of contract proposals or handling media requests. Those things had occupied Marlys's schedule almost full-time, and she had experience that had equipped her for that job. We knew that we didn't.

For weeks we'd been waiting for someone to shut off the spotlight. We were finally beginning to believe what President Clinton had told us, that we would continue to be one of the most watched couples in America for years to come. It was not a welcome prospect.

I vividly remembered how troubled I had been about that "mysterious" car on Thanksgiving Day. I knew we desperately needed someone who would share part of that load that I felt, shield us from unwanted attention, and help us control the world's intrusion into our lives. Ideally that same someone could also enable us to take advantage of those business and endorsement offers that God might use to provide the financial help we would need in order to raise our children.

We asked God to provide us with someone who could help us manage the media and business decisions now facing us.

One morning in early December, we received a phone call from

Wes Yoder, head of the Ambassador Agency in Nashville, Tennessee, a company that specializes in representing Christian clients. When he and Ambassador's vice-president, Ron Miller, flew up to meet us we were impressed. After some prayer, we hired them as our agent—after our initial meetings in our Sunday school classroom at Missionary Baptist Church.

Later that same day, we were scheduled to meet with a nationally recognized tabloid-television journalist who had been pestering us for weeks to do his show. Wes, as our brand-new representative, attended that meeting with us. At the conclusion, he took over, assured the man that we would discuss it, and "if Kenny and Bobbi decide to do your program, we will give you a call." Then he escorted us, graciously, out of the room. I think we all knew we weren't ever going to make that call.

How wonderful, to be able to relax and let an expert handle such situations for us! God had sent a representative who would free us to focus our energy on our family.

Bobbi

Having been abruptly ordered to bed at the nine-week point in my pregnancy, I had not been able to get the house ready for the arrival of our babies. And we had so much to do!

We rented a storage space in town and got busy. We stored Mikayla's crib and got her a "big girl" bed. We moved her new furniture into the smallest bedroom, which had been my sewing room. She helped us fix up that room, just for her. Then we got her old bedroom prepared for the babies. We placed "Moses baskets" around that room for the babies to sleep in when they first came home.

Our rented storage came in handy. We have little closet or attic space in our house and we were given so many things! Articles we wouldn't need for many months, such as bottles, high chairs, rocking horses, and Christmas ornaments, were boxed up and stored there.

Amazingly, even the rented storage wasn't enough. The gifts that poured in filled the fellowship hall at church, several feet high! Many of the presents were handmade; a lot were personalized with the children's names. A number of people thought to also send something for Mikayla.

Determining that we should acknowledge every gift, the church's "McCaughey Committee" formed a subgroup: A "thank-you note committee" took charge of helping me hand-address the more than four thousand notes acknowledging the gifts and mail we received in just the first few months after the septuplets were born. We had to have the notes themselves printed—or we would still be writing personal thank-yous when the babies graduate from high school!

I worried that we were being given too much! Other families had fewer resources than we did; others needed these things more. I called the Alpha Women's Center in Des Moines, a crisis pregnancy agency, and arranged to give them our overflow, the gifts we were unable to use, and our hand-me-downs. I also contacted other mothers of multiples, women with quads and quints, to share our bounty.

People were so generous in their giving to us. I didn't want their generosity to be wasted. We received enough blankets and bibs to supply ten sets of septuplets! I hoped the people around the country who blessed us with their gifts would be happy knowing that their generosity also touched the lives of other families and the mothers at the Alpha Women's Center.

Kenny

Most people having babies come home from the hospital with a small stack of cards and a few plants or flowers stowed in the trunk of their car. By the time they released Bobbi on Sunday, four days after delivery, the hospital had almost an entire loading dock full of gifts and letters. We had to send a truck to haul it all to Carlisle. Most of it went right to the fellowship hall at the church. And that was just the beginning of the deluge of generosity poured out on us.

The post office called us the first of that week. Because there were too many letters for our mail carrier to manage, we had to drive downtown and bring our mail home by the boxful, day after day. And each time we agreed to appear on television like the original *Dateline* interview, which was later updated and expanded into an hour-long Christmas Eve special hosted by Stone Phillips, we could count on an even heavier mail load for several days after the show aired.

We kept wondering when the interest and attention would begin to fade. *Maybe when we finally get the babies all home.*

Bobbi

On Christmas morning, Kenny, Mikayla, and I celebrated together around the tree in our living room. The three of us spent part of the day visiting extended family. Then we headed to the hospital.

That day, the medical team decided to move Nathan out of his isolette and into an open crib—a major step in the eventual homegoing process. Kenny had already been in an open crib for a few days. Kenny, Joel, and Brandon were taking bottles.

I had even been able to nurse Kenny some. I loved the times when I could actually hold a baby to my breast. I wished I could breast-feed all the babies. But I knew I could never produce enough milk to satisfy all the nutritional needs of seven infants. I had been expressing breast milk to be given to the babies through tubes or by bottle. I knew that my milk would help them grow and give them important immunities they couldn't get from formula.

I had started keeping my journal again. On December 25 I reported on the highlight of my Christmas by saying:

> The most exciting thing to happen is that we had our first
> family picture taken. It took quite a while to get everyone
> dressed and into place. But it was worth it.

The babies were doing so well, so much better than anyone had expected. Yet I didn't feel that they were "mine" yet. They seemed to belong more to the nurses.

The members of the medical team were wonderful about reporting on what progress the babies were making and sharing cute stories with us. But even that intensified the disconcerting realization that these other people knew my own children better than I did.

That was tough for me as a mother. If I'd known how long I'd have to deal with those feelings, I'm not sure how well I would have coped.

Nineteen

Under One Roof

Bobbi

My journal for December 27 reads:

The trips to and from the hospital are getting more difficult.
The kids have been there for 5 ½ weeks. At first, going up there
all the time was kind of a novelty. But that has changed. I need
them here at home with me. That will have to be easier than
making trips up there every day.

Each day, we would have good news about the health and
progress of our babies. Kenny was removed from all monitors and
feeding tubes. Brandon breast-fed successfully. I got to give
Kenny a bath. Kelsey took her first bottle, sucking the whole
thing down in no time. Nathan finally nursed. Joel breast-fed the
next day, the same day I was able to give him a bath. On
December 28, I wrote in my journal:

The only one who is still giving us any worry is Alexis. She had to go back up in her oxygen to 33%. And her steroids will be continued for a while yet. They were supposed to end tomorrow. It's this chronic lung disease that keeps tripping her up . . . She was put back on the prayer chain this evening. I pray that God heals her little lungs soon.

Kenny

Bobbi was asked to be a part of one of those year-in-review television specials that always seem to crop up between Christmas and New Year's. After *Dateline* aired she told Wes, our agent, that she didn't really want to do any more TV interviews. However, knowing what the Bible says about the importance of Christians sharing their faith with others, she decided this might be another great opportunity to talk about and honor God. She reconsidered.

The show, produced by *Ladies' Home Journal,* highlighted some of the year's "Most Fascinating Women." I tried to assure Bobbi she'd been on my personal most fascinating women list for several years in a row. It was interesting to realize the rest of the world was now thinking of her in the same light as the other women featured in the show—people such as Secretary of State Madeleine Albright and Princess Di.

Bobbi's feature actually ran in the prime spot at the very end of the hour. "Obviously they saved the best for last," I told her proudly.

Just as she'd done after the *Dateline* story, Bobbi judged her own performance pretty harshly. She's just too private a person to ever really enjoy such public exposure.

January 3 was a far more positive experience for our family.

Kenny, firstborn of the septuplets, the one nicknamed "Hercules," was finally ready to come home from the hospital.

January 3 was also Mikayla's second birthday. She went shopping and then out to lunch with Grandma and Grandpa McCaughey. We spent the morning checking Kenny out of the NICU and were back in Carlisle before Mikayla got home.

When Mikayla saw her little brother, she squealed with joy and asked to hold him. Bobbi sat her down and put Kenny in her arms. After a bit, he began to fuss. Mikayla gave him one of her doll bottles and he sucked on it. That seemed to thrill her, and we all laughed.

What a joyous day! We could hardly wait for six more homecomings.

Bobbi

The good news just kept coming. On January 5, Joel's feeding tube came out and Kelsey got moved to an open crib. Even Alexis seemed to be doing much better. My journal for that day reports:

> She's been bottling most of her feedings. The charge nurse wants us to do a lot of kangaroo care. That's been proven to really help with weight gain, O2 levels, and getting out of the hospital sooner. I'm so glad to see her improve. She had us all really worried for quite a while. Even though the doctors said they weren't overly concerned, they weren't seeing things from a mother's heart . . . It's such an encouragement to see God working in her tiny body.

Kangaroo care is a new concept for most hospitals. It's where the mom and dad hold a baby, skin to skin, against their chests.

Such tactile contact seems to improve a baby's development. Both Kenny and I began doing kangaroo care with all the babies, but particularly Alexis and Natalie.

Kelsey, who had been the smallest at birth, was the first of the girls to have the feeding tubes and monitors removed and the first to move to an open crib. More good news.

But several days after Kenny came home, I had my first real scare—a sobering reminder of the many challenges ahead. In my journal I wrote:

> Mikayla pulled her first stunt since bringing Kenny home. I went into the bathroom and when I came out, she had gotten him out of his seat and was holding him, like it was the most natural thing in the world. So from now on I'll have to take her with me when I leave the room. Boy, talk about sheer panic. God was watching over them.

The next day we got good news *and* bad news. First the bad: At Kenny's initial post-hospital checkup, we were advised to see a specialist about his eyes, which would probably need surgery. Then the good news: Joel and Brandon should be ready to come home on Sunday afternoon, and Kelsey by the end of the next week.

That day, Thursday, January 8, the babies weights were: Kenny, 5 lbs. 12 oz.; Natalie, 4 lbs. 13 ½ oz.; Alexis, 3 lbs. 11 ½ oz.; Kelsey, 4 lbs. 3 ½ oz.; Nathan, 5 lbs. 8 oz.; Brandon, 5 lbs. ½ oz.; and Joel, 4 lbs. 14 oz.

In my journal I wrote:

> They are all getting so big so fast . . . I know it's best for them to grow quickly to get the fat stores they need. But at the same time, these are my last babies. And instead of them going from

infancy to toddlerhood one at a time, they'll all move at once. So my days of having infants will be over in one shot . . . I kind of wish that part of my life hadn't already come to an end.

The bad news about Kenny got worse. He was suffering from retinopathy of prematurity (ROP), an eye condition common to premature babies. Left untreated it can cause blindness. Both Natalie and Kenny had this problem, but Kenny's eyes were decidedly worse.

Dr. Keech, the specialist we needed to see, was in Iowa City, more than a two hours' drive away. We had to get up at 4:30 A.M. on Friday to make the appointment. He agreed with our doctor in Des Moines that Kenny's left eye was okay for now. However, his right eye needed immediate laser surgery. We scheduled that for January 11—two days later.

We left the hospital in Iowa City and rushed back to Des Moines to get on a plane for a previously scheduled trip to Tennessee. Wes Yoder, our agent, had set up an overnight get-away for Kenny and me. He even arranged for a friend's privately owned jet to pick us up at the Des Moines airport, along with Pastor and Ginny Brown, and Marlys and Dan Popma, so we didn't have to hassle with a regular airline.

Kenny

Mikayla stayed overnight with Grandma Addleman, but baby Kenny flew with us on a whirlwind trip that turned out to be one of the true highlights of our lives. Wes met us in Nashville and drove us out to Franklin for a tour of the Ambassador Agency and a wonderful dinner his wife, Linda, had prepared at their home.

Following the meal we all went to a "barn" Christian music artist Michael W. Smith and his wife had built, which additionally served as a cross between a guest house and a lodge. There we also met singer/songwriter Steven Curtis Chapman, along with Christian musician Buddy Greene, and Steve Green—the recording artist whose rendition of "Household of Faith" inspired Bobbi and me to sing the song at our wedding.

Once all the introductions had been made, we joined these guys and their wives (along with a few of their friends) for hot cider and dessert and an informal time of worship, singing, and praise music shared among friends.

Each of the recording artists sang a song appropriate for the occasion. Wes had evidently told Steve Green about our singing "Household of Faith" for our wedding; he encouraged Bobbi and me to stand and sing it for everyone.

I was game. But Bobbi didn't relish becoming a "bawling idiot," so she refused. When someone suggested I sing instead another Steve Green song, "Children Are a Treasure," I agreed to give it a try. But when I looked out over that small crowd, many of whom were professional recording stars whose music and Christian ministries I'd admired for years, I suddenly had second thoughts.

It took all the nerve I could muster to begin to sing:

Homes ring with echoes of laughter
Long after they've come and gone.
For the memory of a tiny face and playful grin
Still bring a smile
Reminding us again
That children are a treasure from the Lord.

Songs sweetly sung by the cradle
Prayers whispered just before bed
And we taught them Jesus loves you
In a simple song
And we pray they won't forget their whole life long.
That children are a treasure from the Lord.

Chorus:
Those bright and trusting eyes
Seem to take us by surprise
And they seem to see what others older miss.
May the gift of faith they hold
Grow as they grow old
May they always know that God will never let them go.

At six they're beginning school days
Sixteen and they're driving the car.
And at twenty-one we'll let them go on their first date
But of course they'll be in bed by eight.
And just knowing that our children really love the Lord.
Is a faithful parent's passion and reward.

Those bright and trusting eyes
Seem to take us by surprise
And they seem to see what others older miss.
May the gift of faith they hold
Grow as they grow old
May they always know that God will never let them go.

Looking over at Bobbi holding little Kenny, thinking of Mikayla, and picturing the six babies still in the hospital four hundred miles away back in Iowa, I choked up a couple of times. But when I did Steve joined right in to carry the number until I regained enough composure to take up the melody again. By the time I finished I'm not sure there was a dry eye in the barn— including my own.

Afterward Steve Green invited me to join him onstage for a number next time he performed in Iowa. Honored, but more than a little intimidated by his offer, I told him I'd think about it.

I kept wanting to pinch myself the entire evening. Not only was everyone so down-to-earth nice, but they all invited us to come back and stay with them at their homes when we could bring the whole family.

The collective message these new friends had for us was, "Guard your hearts. Keep your motives and your hearts clean. Don't be overly impressed by all of the exciting things happening around you." Good advice we determined to heed.

Saturday morning all the menfolk were invited to singer Michael Card's home for brunch. Contemporary Christian music legend and world-famous guitarist Phil Keaggy stopped by to say hello. When all of us guys got back to Wes's house, where the women had stayed for a brunch of their own, it was time to head back to the airport to fly home.

What a memorable experience!

Bobbi

Reality set in when we arrived home from Tennessee Saturday afternoon. We stopped to see Mikayla before leaving her with my folks for another two nights and driving to Iowa City for baby Kenny's surgery. We got the little guy admitted into the intermediate nursery that evening. Then the two of us spent the night at the Ronald McDonald House near the hospital. The sheer exhilaration of the night before was replaced by apprehension and fear. I wouldn't have slept at all if I hadn't been so emotionally drained by everything that had happened over the previous couple of days.

Sunday morning we walked alongside Kenny's bed to the surgical wing and kissed him good-bye. The procedure took only a half hour. When Dr. Keech came out, he assured us that everything had gone well. By the time we got to the nursery, Kenny was being extubated. They had to remove him from the respirator because he was clawing and fighting the tube so violently. Little Kenny spent one more night in the hospital, under observation. And we spent another night with Ronald. Monday morning we were able to go home to Carlisle with our baby.

We dropped him off with Kenny's stepmother, Val, and drove immediately to the hospital in Des Moines, where we got Joel and Brandon, and headed home again. What a wonderful day! Kenny was recovering well from his apparently successful eye surgery. Joel and Brandon came home for the first time. And we received the news that Kelsey would be released on Wednesday.

I fixed supper that Monday night and had my family over to help celebrate all the wonderful events of a very full weekend.

On January 16, we were ready to celebrate again when we were finally able to bring a girl home from the hospital. Kelsey had a viral illness on Wednesday when we'd first planned to bring her home. But by Friday the sixteenth that infection had cleared up.

Unfortunately, the weather hadn't. For a while we thought we might not even be able to get to the hospital because of the snow. But when the weather broke for a time and the snowplows got out, we headed for Des Moines to get our daughter.

Less than a week later, it was Nathan's turn. In my journal I wrote:

> Dawn (one of our favorite nurses) said he raised his hand and asked if he could go home. It's just like they said. All of a sudden the light goes on and they start doing well with their feedings. Now if only that light would click on for Natalie!

The day we brought Nathan home was an adventure. We had to take Kenny, Joel, Brandon, and Kelsey in for shots. Val and my sister Michele rode in with us and a friend, Lydia Arnett, met us there. When we got ready to leave we had five babies and Mikayla with us. While we were getting the car seats into the van, a crowd began to gather.

"You must be the McCaugheys!"

"How are they all doing?"

"Which one is Hercules?"

We must have put on quite a show. Dawn Kirkman, our friend and nurse, was in the van buckling them in and I was handing the babies to her. We tried to answer a few of the questions as we strapped babies in.

The following Sunday was our first time taking six children to church. When we arrived, people were lined up ready to take a baby! I was lucky to have one myself.

I ended up carrying Joel with me. I gave him a bottle during Sunday school. When he finished, I had him up on my shoulder to burp him. He belched so loudly that everyone at both tables stopped talking and laughed. I told them, "I am *so* glad this isn't a girl, behaving that way."

That Sunday was a milestone for another reason. It was January 25, the babies' original due date. Five of them had actually made it home ahead of schedule. Still, I'd been hoping all of them would be home by now.

Please, Lord, I prayed that day. *Make it soon. I don't know how long I can go on feeling divided like this.* I wanted to be home with my six children; I also needed to be with the two still in the hospital. Whichever place I was, part of me was somewhere else. And that constant tension was slowly draining me.

We kept having small setbacks with both Alexis and Natalie. Natalie was still unable to feed from a bottle. Alexis couldn't seem to get completely off the supplemental oxygen. The hospital would increase her steroids, and she would do better with the oxygen. But when they tried to wean her off the steroids, her need for oxygen would rise.

Even though Kenny and I knew that they were the babies that needed us the most, now it was increasingly difficult to make it to the hospital. In my journal I wrote:

> It's so hard to have them up there still. It takes extra people here to watch the other kids, so I feel bad about that. But I also feel that I'm not being fair to the girls. They both just need a lot of prayer.

On February 9, the doctors began a series of tests on the girls to determine what problems Natalie and Alexis were having with feedings. The end result of the tests was that they both needed surgery to correct a problem with reflux, and they both needed to have gastrostomy tubes with Bard buttons put in. The surgery itself should allow them to feed by bottle, but we could also use the feeding tubes to be sure they got the nutrition they needed. My journal reads:

Kenny was all for it immediately. And I knew it needed to be done, but I was just so terrified . . . I just started praying that all would go well . . . This time is much scarier than when Kenny had his [eye surgery]. I guess it's because the girls seem so much more fragile.

The day of the girls' operations was a day I never want to repeat. I woke up that morning with my stomach churning. I assumed it was just nerves. By the time I left for the hospital, Mikayla had spiked a fever of almost 104 degrees but had no other symptoms. I hated leaving my two-year-old, not knowing what was wrong. But I went to the hospital anyway. In the nursery, I held Natalie and Alexis and talked to them before the nurses came to take Natalie to the OR. As soon as they finished with her, they came for Alexis.

The doctor said that both surgeries went well and he expected the girls to recover fully. I went in and saw them on ventilators again. It was like taking a step back in time to see them on Ohio beds, hooked up to so many machines.

Will we ever be able to take them home?

Kenny

That happy day finally arrived on March 1. One hundred and three days since the septuplets were born. One hundred and three days of travel to and from the hospital. One hundred and three nights of separation. It had seemed like an eternity to live with divided hearts and minds. But the wait was finally over.

What a day of celebration that was! We were finally going to have our whole family together!

At the hospital, there were so many pictures to be taken. We took the first five back with us for a reunion with the NICU staff, who all posed for a group photo with the septuplets. ABC was shooting footage for a "Homecoming" television broadcast scheduled to air as a special edition of their newsmagazine show, *Primetime*. Brooks Kraft, a Sygma agency photographer, was taking pictures for *People* magazine.

Realizing the media also wanted to make a big deal of this milestone day in our family, we had decided to limit the disruption by granting exclusives to one TV network and one magazine. We were still operating under the assumption that we had to give them something or we wouldn't have any control over our lives at all.

But the babies didn't much care for all the picture-taking. Then we waited for all the grandparents to get there to make our grand exit. Bobbi said good-bye to all the nurses we had come to know so well. There were lots of happy hugs and tears for everyone.

All sorts of media lined up outside the hospital to record the special day. I made a brief statement to the press. We all got into the van and headed home. There, ABC had more footage to shoot. Our photographer had more pictures to take.

It wasn't until nine o'clock that night that we were finally alone with our entire family. Bobbi and I sat next to each other on the living room couch, with babies and Mikayla on our laps and finally breathed a deep sigh of relief.

Bobbi

Home alone at last! If only it could have lasted. Two days later, Natalie went back to the doctor with an ear infection and a low-grade fever. Alexis followed her example later that day—only her temperature spiked to 103.8. The doctor wanted to keep Alexis in the hospital, to monitor her lung situation.

I had planned a coming-home party for the girls. When I'd set the date for March 7, I thought I was being cautious. Sadly, the day came and we had to have our homecoming party without Alexis.

In fact, our last little girl did not come home for good until March 12. So it was only then, over five months after I checked into Iowa Methodist Medical Center, that our long hospital ordeal was finally over.

Now we could get on with adjusting to life together at home in Carlisle. And that would present a whole new set of challenges.

Twenty

Lifesavers in a Fishbowl

Bobbi

With everyone at home, we finally felt like a family. And we wanted to begin doing normal family things. We just didn't know how hard that was going to be.

We planned a spring trip to Pella, Iowa, for the annual tulip festival. Kenny and I had gone before and enjoyed Pella's quaint Dutch village atmosphere, with its historic background, windmills, and lovely shops. We had taken Mikayla to the festival when she was four months old and had many wonderful memories from that experience.

The more we talked about going, the more I looked forward to the daylong outing. It sounded like fun and seemed very doable as a first-time family adventure. Since we had been to Pella before, we thought we knew what to expect. We would have a chance to try out our two new four-baby strollers. We planned to put all the babies and Mikayla in the strollers, wander through the tulip gardens, and window-shop up and down Pella's streets. We'd even watch the parade.

When the babies got hungry, we could take them to the local park and have a picnic. We realized the babies might get fussy or tired, but I couldn't foresee any serious problems. Mom and Dad and my brother Dennis were going with us. Surely we'd have enough adult help to see everything went smoothly.

I had no way of anticipating how our new "celebrity" status would change things.

We arrived in Pella after an uneventful one-hour drive. We parked, took the children out of their car seats, and put them into strollers. But as soon as we started down the streets of Pella, people began to take notice.

"Hey, look at all those babies!"

"Haven't I seen you somewhere?"

"You're the McCaugheys, aren't you?"

"Hey, look, there are the septuplets!"

And look they did. So many people crowded around and right in front of us that we had no choice but to stop. They completely blocked our way.

People kept talking, obviously excited and thrilled to see our babies: "They are so beautiful!"

"Look how big they are."

"Which one is Hercules?"

"How are they doing now?"

"Are you in your new house yet? How is that coming?"

In some ways I didn't mind. What mother objects to hearing sweet comments about her babies? I wanted to answer their questions. After all, they were interested in our children. But I didn't know what question to answer first. And I didn't know how to carry on a conversation with so many people all at the same time.

I appreciated their interest, but I felt bombarded by so much attention and so many questions.

Finally, Kenny took charge of the situation. "We're here as a family, not a novelty!" he told the crowd. When he began pushing a stroller forward, people made a path for us. But even walking down the street, we made our way through a moving sea of strangers, all jostling one another and us, eager for a glimpse of our "world-famous" family.

After a few minutes, we realized that the interest in our family was not going to be a short-lived sensation. People were not getting their fill, then going away and leaving us alone. We gave up on the window shopping and headed to the park. Surely there, out in the open, we could find breathing room.

We parked the strollers near a picnic table and began getting bottles out. I thought that once people saw we were feeding babies, they would wander away to enjoy the tulips and the festival.

Instead, you'd have thought we were putting on a show for the benefit of the onlookers—like feeding time for the seals at a zoo. People crowded around to see the special, unadvertised event: the feeding of the septuplets.

Kenny

Finally, it was just too much. We pushed the strollers back to the van, put the children in their car seats, and finished feeding them there. By then it was noon on a warm, sunny spring day. Inside the van was hot and stuffy—hardly the pleasant open-air picnic we'd planned. We left a couple of doors open in an effort to cool off. But people wanted to see our babies and poked their heads into the van, hoping for a close-up peek.

When everyone had eaten, we tried to salvage something of the day. Bobbi and her mother put the children into the strollers, and we headed back into downtown Pella to watch the parade. It was the babies' naptime, and they fell asleep in their strollers almost as soon as we started.

We'd forgotten to bring sunscreen. So we draped blankets across the tops of the strollers to keep the babies shaded and to help them sleep. No sooner had we started walking than the crowd pressed in around us again. Tourists lifted the blankets off the strollers, just to look at our babies!

I wondered whether anyone would care if we mowed the tulips down with our strollers. We had come to see the tulips, but felt as if we had ended up being the tulips.

We stayed in Pella until about 2:00 P.M., then gave up and headed home. We hadn't been able to relax, window-shop, picnic, or do much of anything fun. By the time we left, I was so frustrated, I felt sick and my head ached. Mostly, I felt sad. Bobbi and I had always enjoyed doing things like this. *How are we ever going to be able to have family outings? Our kids shouldn't have to miss out on such things, just because of who they are!*

In the press conference the day after our babies arrived, when asked about my hopes and fears, I'd said, "Our big fear is that this not turn into a big show . . . We are not on display."

We appreciated everyone's interest in our family. The same interest had prompted so many people to write us, pray for our family, and shower us with gifts. We were grateful for the interest people had shown us and our children. And we understood that the people visiting Pella that day were just excited to see us and intrigued by the sight of so many babies. But we were at a loss to know how to deal with all their well-meaning interest.

Bobbi

We'd already experienced some of that celebrity phenomenon, but in smaller measures, just by going out to restaurants to eat. Usually, someone recognized us and spoke to us by name. Sometimes we got seated at better tables or received better service because we'd been recognized. A couple of times restaurant owners had given us our meals free, and that was nice.

People have been extremely generous with us. In fact, we have been overwhelmed by the generosity of others. We received gifts in the mail, almost every day, from ordinary people who wanted to share with us. Many companies donated products our family needs and uses on a regular basis. More than one hundred companies participated in the building of our house. God used the generosity of many people to shower us with blessings. He was faithful in His promise to "supply all our need according to His riches in glory."

Kenny

People were indeed generous with their time and effort as well as with their money. Once all the babies were out of the hospital, our lives at home began to fall into something of a routine. But it was a schedule we could never have maintained by ourselves.

The church's McCaughey Committee had discussed the assistance we would need once the babies came home. Ginny Brown, our pastor's wife, with the help of other women from our church, set up a McCaughey Volunteer Schedule. As soon as we had three babies at home, we had help overnight, every night. And by the time Nathan came home on January 21, we had two to four people helping us at home, in four- to six-hour shifts, around the clock.

Between volunteer shifts, Bobbi and I had two hours alone with the children each morning, from 6:00 A.M. to 8:00 A.M. On Saturday afternoon and all day Sunday, we managed by ourselves.

The rest of the time, we had more than seventy regular helpers, taking their turns. Ginny gave us a monthly schedule to po st on our refrigerator, showing who was signed up for which shift. Most of our helpers took the same four-or six-hour shift each week.

Ginny held a training session for our volunteers. She and Bobbi showed everyone our feeding schedules, discussed how to feed the babies and what to mark on each chart, and answered questions about the care of our children. And Ginny reminded the helpers that this was our house and that these were Bobbi's and my children. They were asked to respect the ways we did things with the children.

All our volunteers were given courses (taught by medical professionals) in preemie care and infant CPR to help them be prepared for dealing with premature babies. Ginny even scheduled extra helpers on Friday evenings so that Bobbi and I could go out on dates. We often just took that time to go over to Dad and Val's to watch a video, or to Bobbi's folks to visit. That time was invaluable for maintaining our marriage. As Ginny told us, the best gift we could give our eight children was for our marriage to stay strong.

Bobbi

The volunteers were absolutely essential. I quickly discovered that although I could hold three babies at once, I couldn't feed three at the same time. But with our helpers, we always had extra arms to hold babies, extra people around to play with or read to Mikayla. Part of me wished that every time my babies or my two-year-old needed something, I could be the one to meet that need. I knew that simply wasn't possible.

I felt grateful that I could see my children being held, fed, and comforted by friends and neighbors who cared enough to give us their time and energy. And they gave faithfully, cheerfully, over the long haul. Most of them had been with us week after week, month after month, from the beginning and promised they'd be with us as long as we need them. They saw their work as a true ministry of love, a gift to God as well as to us. What a humbling thing that was to be a part of!

We even had friends who covered the night shift for us. Kenny and I regularly slept through the night, long before the babies did. I often awoke if I heard a baby cry in the night. But I could go back to sleep knowing that my baby's needs were being attended to. Sometimes the crying would continue and I would stumble out and comfort the fussy one. Most nights that wasn't necessary.

I perhaps could have survived alone during the days. But not without those good nights of rest. I'm glad I never had to try it alone. Not with four hundred dirty diapers and nearly that many bottles a week, plus all the baths and the changes of clothes, not to mention all the hugs and kisses doled out, all the lullabies sung, and all the assorted other things children need to feel loved and comforted.

Kenny

The downside of our need for volunteers, though, was the lack of privacy. We felt as though we had company in our home all the time. They were people we loved, friends we needed. But after a while anyone gets tired of having company every day, all day long. When I came home from work, I couldn't let my hair down and tell Bobbi if I'd had a bad day. If I woke up in the night, I had to dress before I could go across the hall to the bathroom. To have a private conversation, we had to retreat to our bedroom or wait until our weekly date night.

One Friday evening, after only about two weeks of full-time help, Bobbi and I left for our night out and just drove around Carlisle. We started talking about how we missed our privacy, and the next thing we knew we had to pull off the street beside a grain elevator to hold each other and cry.

That was probably the low point. After a few short weeks, we adjusted. I realized that all the people were there to help us out of the goodness of their hearts. They could surely understand if I came home grumpy after a hard day. That helped me relax and appreciate our volunteers even more.

I don't know how we would have survived without our faithful, cheerful, irreplaceable company. They were our lifesavers.

In addition to helping us around the house with our children, our friends and neighbors were great about treating us like a normal family. Carlisle was the one place where our celebrity status didn't seem to change our lives. Late spring and early summer brought church softball games. Last summer, with Bobbi pregnant, had been the first year that I hadn't played on our church softball team. By the summer of 1998, I was ready to get back in the swing of things. On game days, we loaded the children into their strollers and headed for the park. As we walked by, neighbors out in their yards would look up, smile, and say, "Hi!" But we never had to worry about being mobbed.

When we arrived at the games, friends from church would volunteer to hold babies or play with Mikayla. Bobbi sat in the stands, watching while my dad and I pitched. She cheered for us and talked with people. It felt wonderful to enjoy such normal family excursions.

Almost daily, Bobbi and I and the kids would walk around the corner to see what progress had been made on our new house. Occasionally, we'd take the family to a local restaurant to eat out. And in Carlisle people smiled and waved, but they allowed us to live pretty much as we always have.

Bobbi

Being able to live a normal life in Carlisle helped a lot, since some parts of our lives seemed anything but normal. Each time a news show or magazine wanted an interview, I dreaded it. I really didn't like talking to the media. Each time we had the opportunity, Kenny reminded me that we had an obligation to talk to others about our faith. The Bible tells us to go into all the world (Matthew 28:19). We'd never before thought we'd actually speak to "the world." But each interview was a chance to share our faith with more people than we had ever before dreamed possible.

So we were interviewed for *Life, People, Ladies' Home Journal,* and other magazines. We appeared on not only local television but also national programs such as *Dateline* and *ABC Primetime.* Each time we spoke to the media, we tried to give witness to the glory of God.

In spite of my personal aversion to being so public, our media experiences were often wonderful. Some of our interviewers, such as Peggy Wehmeyer of ABC News, were not only warm and caring, but sympathetic and affirming when we talked about our faith. In the course of our contact with Peggy, we became friends.

Kenny

While the overall tone of most media coverage had been over-whelmingly positive, we had received enough criticism and judg-ment that both Bobbi and I soon approached each new media opportunity a little wary. We took interviews because we truly wanted to give the glory to God. And after each article or show, we would receive mail from people whose lives had been touched by our story, some of whom turned to God after hearing about our faith. Those letters were gratifying.

Yet each media appearance also brought its share of negative reactions. We read newspaper and magazine articles that criti-cized our use of fertility drugs, saying that our babies were results of medical technology: How dare we call them miracles of God.

We received critical letters from people who did not under-stand us or what our lives were like. One such letter was from a woman who had sent us seven afghans. After we appeared on one network news show, she wrote that her feelings had been hurt that we hadn't shown her handmade blankets on television. We appreciated the outpouring of love and generosity demonstrated by so many folks. But we could hardly single out one or two gifts to a national audience.

Sometimes we were criticized by people who didn't know us at all. We read articles by psychologists or other so-called experts who passed judgment on us or predicted emotional trauma for our children. Those were easier to shrug off: We knew they didn't know what they were talking about. As Bobbi said on ABC's homecoming special, some of the psychotherapists asked to publicly comment on our lives not only didn't know us, "They probably couldn't find Carlisle, Iowa, on a map."

Occasionally, we were judged for things we didn't even do. We received one particularly condemning letter that complained: In appearing on television with David Letterman we'd obviously sold out our faith in what had become a publicity-hungry quest for fame. What our letter-writing critic didn't know was that we had never been on Letterman's show and we had turned down an invitation to do so!

All in all, being unable to go out in public without drawing sometimes overwhelming attention, living with a houseful of company twenty-four hours a day for month after month, being watched by millions of people and sometimes questioned and criticized about the way we chose to live our lives, we often felt as though we were living in a fishbowl.

Our new life seemed open to inspection from every side. Which meant the new life we were living seemed very different from the one we'd had before November of 1997.

Bobbi

Life seemed a lot fuller now. And with eight small children, our lives at home were certainly a lot busier. But never so full or so busy that we failed to notice and appreciate the remarkable progress our babies were making.

In June we celebrated a major milestone: Alexis finally went off oxygen. She had been the smallest and the one most bothered by the lung disease that commonly affects premature babies. For weeks after she'd come home from the hospital she'd been hooked to a monitor twenty-four hours a day and been receiving the smallest dose of oxygen the machine could deliver—a barely perceptible whiff of oxygen was all she needed to bolster each breath she took on her own. But she clearly did need that little bit of help because anytime we removed the tiny tube from her nose for a few minutes—to bathe her or move her to another location—an alarm would sound on the monitor that constantly measured the oxygen saturation of her blood.

Then one day in June, I gave her a bath and forgot to turn the oxygen back on after bath time. The monitor never sounded, meaning Alexis's oxygen count was fine, and it was afternoon before I stopped to realize, *Wow! Alexis hasn't needed her oxygen all day.* Over the next few days I turned off the oxygen during the day, but left it on during the night when Alexis was sleeping. Before the month was over, our littlest angel was completely weaned off any supplemental oxygen. We continued to monitor her periodically to be safe, but it was wonderful not to have to hassle with tubes and wires every time we picked Alexis up.

By midsummer the only significant ongoing medical concern was feeding Natalie and Alexis. Neither of them has been able to suck enough from a bottle to fill her nutritional needs. While that's fairly common among preemies and was easily solved in the hospital as long as they were hooked up to IVs, it did present a problem when they came home.

Alexis actually had a little better sucking reflex than Natalie did. But it became obvious even in the hospital that neither of them was going to get the food she needed that way. That's why we went ahead with the operations to insert their G-tubes with Bard buttons. The doctors assured us that many babies go right from tube feedings to drinking from a cup and eating solid foods. They didn't see the tubes as a major or lasting concern.

Also in June we started Kenny, Joel, Nathan, Kelsey, and Brandon on soft foods like applesauce and cereal. Natalie and Alexis followed suit in July. We're hopeful that by the time the other kids no longer need bottles, Natalie and Alexis will no longer need any shortcuts to their stomachs and will be drinking from cups, with the rest of their siblings.

In the meantime, it's great to know all seven babies are getting all the nourishment they need. They're growing faster than a field of Iowa corn in July. At their nine-month checkup their weights ranged from Joel at 17 lbs. even down to Alexis at 10 lbs. 12 oz. Dr. Pete Hetherington, our pediatrician, smiled and shook his head as he told us he would be hard-pressed to pick another seven nine-month-olds from his practice who were as healthy as our septuplets.

Despite their prematurity, our babies were developing on schedule—gurgling, smiling, laughing, grasping, and playing like other children their age. They were scooting and rolling over to reach one another and to get where they wanted to go by summertime. We began to hope and pray we'd be able to move into our new and bigger house before all seven of them were walking. We seemed to be cutting it close.

All the doctors remained absolutely amazed at the babies' good health and our good fortune. We were just very grateful.

And not just that our babies were doing so miraculously well. But also for the interest, the prayers, the love, and the help of all those wonderful people who have followed, and shared in, our lives these past few months.

Twenty-One

Happy Campers Again

Kenny

For a long while only the chirping of crickets broke the silence surrounding me. I still didn't sleep very well on the first night of a camping trip. Slowly, I began to tune in to other, subtler night sounds.

Lying awake in the darkness, I listened to the familiar sound of my wife's breathing as she snuggled next to me in the cozy cocoon of our two zipped-together sleeping bags in the center of our three-room cabin tent. Beyond Bobbi, on the far side of the thin nylon partition, I could just barely make out the soft stirrings of thirty-two-month-old Mikayla as she shifted restlessly, sprawled out under a blanket on top of a quilt. Beside her, lying in a row in a playpen and wrapped snugly in baby blankets were Mikayla's three sisters—Kelsey, Natalie, and Alexis. On the side nearest me, opposite the girls, in the third room of the tent, were all four boys—Joel, Brandon, Nathan, and little Kenny—all asleep, for now, on the first night of the very first camping trip of their nine-month-old lives.

Outside a gentle breeze softly rustled the leaves high in the trees that lined the perimeter of our campsite and brought some relief to what had been an unseasonably hot and muggy day. Inside, lying awake, enjoying once again the sensation of life under the stars, I couldn't help thinking back to our last camping experience on that fateful Memorial Day weekend at Jester State Park. As my tense, but tired, body slowly wound down and I waited for sleep, my mind wandered back over so much that had happened in the fifteen months since that outing.

Bobbi

We'd gotten a variety of reactions from people who learned we planned to take Mikayla and all seven babies camping over the long Labor Day weekend:

"You don't mean this year, 1998, do you?"

"Really? No kidding?"

"Wow! You're awfully brave to try that!"

"Well . . . good luck!"

Some people didn't say anything; they just shook their heads. I feel certain most people were thinking (even if they were too polite to say it), *Bobbi and Kenny must be crazy. The pressure of having septuplets has gotten to them and they've finally cracked.*

I'm not sure I reassured any doubters with my response. Whenever family or friends expressed surprise or doubt about the plan, I smiled and said, "Why not?"

Of course I knew it would be a lot of work to take care of a toddler and seven babies on a camping trip. But it's not exactly a walk in the park at home every day, either. And I figured the fun, the adventure, and the chance to do something together that Kenny and I have always enjoyed would more than compensate for the hassle.

Happy Campers Again

Taking our expanded family camping took a bit more planning and a lot more packing than a holiday weekend used to require. With so many packages of diapers, formula and bottles, baby food and bowls, four days' worth of clothes for all kinds of weather, plus a small mountain of piled up baby blankets, we needed all the space we could find in our new big white extended van. Once we got our two four-seat strollers mounted on the luggage racks atop the van, I suspect we looked every bit as weighed down and prepared for adventure in the "wilderness" as any pioneer family rolling through the Midwest in a Conestoga wagon a century and a half ago.

Between taking care of the kids and going through the normal daily routines, I'd spent most of my time and energy that Friday finishing the packing and rechecking my lists of everything we were going to need for the weekend. The van was loaded and ready to go at six that evening when Kenny got home from work. Once he changed clothes, all we had to do was strap eight kids into their car seats and we were off.

As expected at the start of the summer's last holiday weekend, rush-hour traffic was heavy in and around Des Moines. But we hadn't worried because this time Neil and Barbara had made reservations for all of us at a private campground on Saylorville Lake only an hour's drive or so from Carlisle. We'd known whatever time we arrived, there would be a spot waiting for us to set up our tent—on a campsite equipped with electricity and running water this time—within sight of a bathroom containing showers and flush toilets. With so many comforts of home it hardly seemed like camping.

Neil and Barbara were already set up when we arrived; they had their three kids with them. Pete and Linda had arrived with their little one. To improve the adult-child ratio, Mom, Dad, and my youngest brother, Dennis, came for the weekend and were staying with Pete and Linda's family. Kenny's Dad and Val also volunteered to share our adventure and brought along Matt and Alisha. Altogether we had fifteen kids and ten adults. So I was anticipating a lot of experienced and loving help to get us through what promised to be a weekend we would all remember forever.

Why not?

So far so good. We got all twelve little ones down for bed that first night of the trip with much less difficulty than our doubters could ever have imagined. And we hadn't attracted a crowd this time out.

People around the campground certainly noticed us. How could anyone not notice so many young children at one campsite? But only two men come over, and they merely wished us well and commented on what good campers the babies seemed to be.

Once the children were asleep, we adults sat around the camp-fire or the picnic table, talking, playing games, and just enjoy-ing one another's company. Some of the guys agreed to go fishing early the next morning. But most of us planned to sleep in as long as the children would let us.

As the evening progressed and the temperature dropped to a more comfortable level, everyone there had been reminded of the last big family camping weekend over Memorial Day more than a year before. Lying beside Kenny in our sleeping bag in the quiet darkness of our tent, I, too, was thinking about everything that had happened since then.

Kenny

We'd been anticipating another camping trip for months. We talked about it close to Memorial Day. But Alexis was on oxygen.

And Bobbi thought things would go better if we could wait until all the babies were sleeping through the night on a regular basis. So Labor Day weekend became our target date. In retrospect I had to admit it had been wise to wait. Because lying there in our tent, I realized there were a lot of reasons, in addition to the recent positive medical reports, why we'd been able to approach this camping trip with excitement and optimism about the weekend.

For one thing, we already had a far more imposing trip under our belts. Over the Fourth of July, when the babies had been seven and a half months old, I had taken a week off work and we'd driven to Michigan for a ten-day vacation.

Bobbi's mom, dad, and Dennis went with us then too. We'd loaded the kids in the van as soon as I got off work on Thursday evening, July 2, and drove through the night across Iowa, Illinois, Indiana, and up into Michigan. We reached Bobbi's grandparents' home near Owosso a little before sunup. The babies pretty much slept through the night, but Mikayla was so excited, she was wired. While the seven little ones stayed right on their regular schedules, the rest of us took a day or two to get back up to par.

Bobbi

Every summer Saturday morning Grandpa and Grandma Hepworth go to a local farmers' market to sell cut flowers and vegetables they grow in their gardens. They wanted us to take the kids so they could show off their great-grandchildren to their vendor friends and regular customers.

I'd been leery of taking all the kids anywhere out in public (besides church) ever since our experience at the tulip festival in Pella. But grandparents are . . . well . . . grandparents. I loved and wanted to please them. With more than a little fear and trepidation we strapped the strollers on top of the van and all eight kids in their car seats and took them all to market.

Grandma and Grandpa were thrilled to see us drive up. Their friends were impressed, and our crop of babies did create quite a stir among the vegetable stands that morning. But the crowds were manageable. People were friendly and polite. By the time we left the market I was actually glad we'd come. In part because it was a positive public experience, but mostly because I knew how much it meant to my grandparents, who'd always meant so much to me.

All in all our time in Michigan proved to be a relaxing family vacation. My parents and I spent a little time driving Kenny around and showing him some places important in our family history—where I'd lived, played, gone to church, and attended school growing up. But most of our time was spent right there in my grandparents' old farmhouse, visiting with them and with the stream of aunts and uncles and cousins who dropped by to see us.

We took one all-day outing across the state to the beautiful little harbor town of Pentwater on the Lake Michigan shore of the Lower Peninsula. The extended Hepworth clan had a big annual reunion picnic there that day with distant relatives gathering from all over Michigan and the Midwest. I hadn't been back for that reunion in years, so Kenny and the kids met shirttail cousins I hadn't seen in ages.

We all had a wonderful afternoon sitting and talking around picnic tables in the shade of a pavilion shelter in a park overlooking the white-capped waves rolling in off the deep blue water of Lake Michigan. But even in that peaceful, beautiful setting among family, things were public enough that I couldn't completely relax. I found myself constantly looking around and counting babies. On the way back to Owosso that evening, Dad admitted he'd done the same thing.

However, when we weren't out in a public setting, we could all relax. And we did a lot of that during our vacation. While the kids demanded just as much of our time as they do at home, the different setting and the chance to be with people we love made it a refreshing change of pace. We made the long trip home after ten days, encouraged by the experience and hopeful that we could expect to have even more positive outings with the entire family in the years ahead.

Kenny

Later that month we had a different kind of encouraging experience when we took Mikayla and the babies to another memorable picnic. It was sponsored by the central Iowa chapter of Mothers of Multiples, a local support group for families with triplets or more. The cookout was held in Boone, Iowa, at the home of Mary and Grant Gustofson, who are parents of two-year-old quadruplets and eight-year-old Scottie. Mary and three other mothers of multiples had visited Bobbi in the hospital before our babies were born—to offer encouragement and answer any questions.

Since our babies' births, Bobbi has been in touch with the group—passing along some of the clothing and gifts our kids had outgrown or we couldn't use. And Bobbi has attended one or two of their regular meetings. So she knew some of the moms who were there.

They were all strangers to me. But I met some interesting folks and had a good time anyway. It was an interesting crowd with our eight kids, three sets of quads, one set of triplets, and some expectant quad parents.

Ours were some of the youngest sets of multiples there. So when I looked around at the herd of kids toddling, running, and playing in that backyard, I envisioned a little of what our lives will be like in the months and years ahead.

It made me extremely glad that our new house is going to have a fenced backyard. It added to my anticipation and longing for the day our kids would be old enough that we could take care of them ourselves and not need to depend on our round-the-clock volunteers.

Bobbi

In that regard we reached a major milestone sooner than a lot of people expected. As of the first of August, with all seven babies regularly sleeping through the night, Kenny and I decided to release our night-shift volunteers.

Those good folks had donated one night a week of their time for months on end. They were lifesavers. I don't know how we could have survived—physically or emotionally—without their selfless service. We developed many special relationships that we cherish and hope to maintain in new and different ways.

From eight o'clock every evening until eight o'clock the next morning, Kenny and I were now alone in our house with our children. Not only did we relish the sense of privacy we'd recaptured after so many months of constant company, we'd begun to look ahead and form a clearer, more realistic picture of a time when our home will once again be a sanctuary from the world, a private place of peace, a safe haven to retreat for rest and restoration.

Both Kenny and I believed our new house would be a big step in the right direction. We would finally have enough room to allow some privacy even inside the house. Two full floors with a finished basement plus a garage almost as big as our entire house on First Street promised space to get away and think, be alone, or quietly retreat from the constant commotion for a time without having to leave the house. Even when we had company and helpers in the house, there could be entire floors where we could go to let down and be ourselves or to carry on conversations that couldn't be overheard.

Lying in the tent that hot September evening, I experienced again the mixed feelings I always had when I thought about our future home. On the one hand, I felt a very real sense of awkwardness, to be given such a wonderful home that we'd really done nothing to deserve or earn. On the other hand, I had more anticipation and excitement than I could sometimes contain and an overwhelming thankfulness that no words could adequately express. It was humbling and wonderful all at the same time. When I thought about all our new house will mean to the future of our family, I could hardly wait to move in.

Kenny

We are well aware that we will face some incredible challenges—financial and otherwise—in the years ahead. But we have been so blessed by God and by the generosity of so many people He has used to help meet our needs to this point. As a result, we're optimistic and confident that God will continue to provide us the energy, the resources, and the assistance we need to raise the children He in His infinite wisdom has given us.

If we aren't careful, it would be easy to obsess over some of the ominous predictions from "experts" who estimate it will cost us $10 million to raise our children and see them through college.

Should it cost us only a third, a fourth, or even a tenth of that, we're going to have to trust God to provide. There is no way I will ever earn that kind of money working at my job. If we stay in Carlisle as we're determined to do, there are very limited opportunities for landing another job that will pay a lot more money.

I guess that is one reason so many people seemed surprised that we turned down almost $1 million from a tabloid that wanted exclusive rights to our story. But as Bobbi explained our thinking to ABC's Peggy Wehmeyer when she interviewed us for the homecoming special, "There's no amount of money that is worth having your reputation destroyed or your integrity damaged. And that could happen with a single article."

We'd determined from the beginning that our babies were not for sale, and neither were we.

That hasn't meant we turned down every business opportunity offered us. It just means we want to be careful about which ones we accept. For example, Bobbi signed a contract with Simplicity to endorse a line of clothing patterns for moms, babies, and toddlers. She'd spent several days earlier in the summer selecting and approving the various patterns for the line. Then she'd worked with a photographer many long hours over two straight days getting promotional pictures of Bobbi, Mikayla, and the babies for use in marketing and advertising. For Bobbi, as a longtime seamstress, it was a special thrill to think about seeing her own name and the smiling images of her children in the Simplicity catalog and on the pattern packages.

I'd gotten an appealing endorsement opportunity of my own during the summer when Black and Decker contacted our agent to ask if I'd be willing to appear in an ad for a snazzy new cordless power drill scheduled to go on the market in time for the Christmas 1998 shopping season. The company had an advertising spot planned to show me as a typical handyman Dad, wielding the new product while working on a variety of home projects for my kids—from installing a long row of clothes hooks behind a bathroom door to assembling an impressive backyard swing set big enough to accommodate all my children.

My longest line, delivered after I finished putting together my seventh high chair and then turned to survey all my handiwork, was: "I think we're gonna need a bigger house."

I flew to New York City with our agent, Wes Yoder, where we spent an entire weekend filming take after take for one short commercial spot. The experience had been fun and crazy at the same time. I'd gotten two memorable days experiencing the life of a "professional actor," and I'd had my first-ever trip to New York City where forty-eight hours had been more than enough to make me extremely grateful I would soon be going home to Carlisle, Iowa.

While I was lying in the dark inside our tent on the shores of an Iowa lake on Labor Day weekend, those memories of the bright lights and the big city seemed from another world. I had no idea what, if any, other endorsement and business opportunities might come our way in the future. But Bobbi and I determined we aren't going to accept any offers that don't fit with who we are and who we've always been.

Bobbi

Just a couple of weeks before our Labor Day camping trip, Kenny had one opportunity that probably excited him as much as anything that has happened since our babies were born. Steve Green came to Des Moines for a concert, and just as he'd promised back in January, he invited Kenny to sing with him.

We arrived early for the Friday night concert at one of the

biggest churches in downtown Des Moines. Kenny and I went backstage a few minutes ahead of time to confirm the plan and to pray with Steve before the concert began. Then we settled back in our front row seats to enjoy the music.

A few minutes into the concert Steve Green called Kenny up on the stage, introduced him, and asked him to sing "Children Are a Treasure." I don't know how Kenny managed that in front of such a big crowd. But he did. And I would have been proud even if the audience hadn't responded so warmly.

Then during intermission, Steve summoned Kenny backstage again, and they practiced a duet to sing later in the program. Before the concert was over, Kenny went back up on stage and joined one of our all-time favorite musicians in concert to sing the old Christian hymn "It Is Well with My Soul."

What a thrill and an honor that was for Kenny! He'd been nervous for weeks ahead of time—wanting so badly to accept the opportunity and fulfill such a dream—but not at all confident he could pull it off without embarrassing himself. When the whole evening came off so beautifully Kenny was so excited that I knew the memory of that evening will always be considered one of the true highlights of his life.

I have a very different attitude toward opportunities involving large crowds. I'd already turned down one offer someone sent to our agent asking me to speak to an audience of twelve thousand at a women's conference. I laughed and told Wes, "No way!"

My reaction has little to do with the size of the crowd. I just know I'm not a public speaker. Maybe someday, when the kids are older, I'll have grown to the point that I'll be willing and able to share my experience and the lessons I'm learning with others in a formal public setting. But right now I have more than enough to do just being a mom. What creative and emotional energies I have, what communication skills I may possess, I intend to devote to my children and my family.

Kenny

We know a lot of people wonder, with Bobbi's dislike of cameras and public speaking, and both our concerns about the often uncomfortable downside of public attention (especially the loss of privacy), why have we agreed to do so many things in the national media? Why all the magazine cover stories? Why so many network television interviews? Aren't we being inconsistent when we talk about wanting a normal family life for our kids at the same time we agree to endorse certain products and appear on prime-time television specials?

We're constantly asking ourselves some of those same questions because we are determined not to do anything that would exploit our children, betray ourselves and our values, or dishonor God. There are three major reasons we've accepted some of the opportunities that have come our way.

First, we still believe in the basic media strategy that we embraced from the beginning. We now realize the spotlight isn't going to go off anytime soon. If we grant interviews with a few reporters or publications we feel good about, if we agree to appear on certain programs we select, we can control much of the attention our kids receive and actually limit the amount of intrusion into our family's life. And we also now know that some opportunities we accept can lead directly to other opportunities (such as Bobbi's Simplicity Patterns line and my Black and Decker power drill endorsements) that will enable us to provide for the needs of our children without compromising our family or our faith.

The second major reason we've accepted some media opportunities is that we feel a sense of obligation to the public for their prayers and support, and we also feel a sense of tremendous gratitude for the generosity so many individuals and groups have shown us. It would seem terribly selfish to say, "Thanks for everything, but we have nothing to say. Please leave us alone." Articles and interviews give us a chance to express our gratitude, to thank the public, and to give a little of ourselves back to all those people who've given so much to us. There have been far too many people to ever include in our lives in person. But if they get to know us a little bit by reading an article or watching us on TV, maybe they'll see our appreciation and sense the impact of so many people's generosity on our lives.

The third reason we've continued to work with the media interested in our story is perhaps the simplest. It's certainly the most important reason in our minds. We've already talked a little about it. As Christians, we take seriously the Bible's instruction that all believers are to take responsibility for sharing the good news of God's love with others.

We've been given an extraordinary platform. We didn't choose to have seven babies. But because we did have them, people around the world have taken an interest in us and are watching us. As Christians, we have a God-given responsibility to let others know what He has done and what He is doing in our lives. The media opportunities we are given allow us to witness about our faith, and to share the lessons God is still teaching us, with millions of people at once.

Before long we're hoping to use our public platform to do more than talk. We're exploring the possibilities of giving some of our time and energies to help raise money and resources for organizations working with needy families and children around the world. We've had so much given to us that we want to channel the public's generosity toward others. To think that we can have that kind of impact and ministry is one more humbling and exciting by-product of everything that has happened to us this past year and a half.

Bobbi

We have learned, indeed we're still learning, so much we feel we need and want to share:

We've learned a lot about dependency—on others and on God. As a parent, as a human being, no one of us is intended to have to go it alone. We need to get past our pride, admit our needs, and depend on God to show His love and care for us—often through the people He's placed around us.

We're learning to be more open with others. By making ourselves more vulnerable, we open ourselves to relationship opportunities we would otherwise never have had.

Kenny and I have learned to value our relationship, our marriage, and what time we have together. The bits and pieces of time we are able to share together mean more to us now than they ever did.

We're constantly learning what we only thought we knew before—that parenting requires very real sacrifice—but that the rewards far exceed the demands. We're learning to enjoy our kids even as we sometimes struggle to meet their constant needs. We have experienced the truth of what I told Peggy Wehmeyer when she asked how we thought we could possibly meet all the emotional requirements of eight children. When God created the miracle of love, He gave it an amazing characteristic our human minds can't truly fathom. The love

God created, the love He shares with us and wants us to share with others, is infinitely expandable. Love grows to fit the need.

We loved Mikayla with all our hearts when she was our only child; there was no more love to give her. But when our seven babies were born, God expanded the love in our hearts so that we could love each one of them just as much. That amazing love, God's love, originating with Him and shared with us to share with others, is the greatest miracle of all. And we're still learning and seeing what that means in our lives.

Kenny

We're also learning the importance of prayer as God's support system—not just as a source of strength and encouragement for making it through each day, but as a means of guidance in making all the new and difficult decisions we encounter in a life that seems suddenly far more complicated than we imagined possible a couple of years ago.

Most important, I think, has been learning to trust God. Sometimes we haven't had much choice. But He's proven Himself worthy of that trust again and again.

That doesn't mean we believe God will somehow magically make everything turn out the way we would like. It doesn't meant life will always be easy or bad things won't happen. We know it certainly doesn't mean everything will always go as well as it has so far for our children and our family.

But we are learning that no matter what happens today, tomorrow, or sometime in the future, God will be here with us. And we can trust Him to help us face whatever happens—good or bad.

That assurance enables me to fall asleep at night, even on the first night of our first big family camping trip.

Bobbi

It's also why I wake up every morning feeling optimistic and able to face whatever the day will bring. Even in the dim light of dawn, in a tent surrounded by eight babies, each of whom had been up at least once in the night, on Saturday morning of a long Labor Day weekend, realizing we have our work cut out for us.

This time, I heard no rain. I felt no pain. It was another hot day for camping, but the sky seemed almost as bright as the future.

Conclusion

The Household of Faith

Kenny and Bobbi

*D*uring our very first press conference after the births of our babies a reporter asked us, "Do you realize yet what you've got ahead of you?"

We've lost track of the times we've heard variations on that question since. How will you cope? Where will the necessary energy come from? What will it cost? In other words, "Do you have any idea what it's going to take to raise septuplets?"

Our answer to that is, "We're learning." Truth is, whether we have one or two or seven or eight children, we as parents can never know what lies ahead of us. All parents struggle with the expectations, the demands, and the awesome responsibility we face. We all have to learn as we go—some faster, some slower, than others.

Much has been made in recent years of the old African saying: It takes a village to raise a child.

We've learned that a village certainly can help. Friends and neighbors in our village of Carlisle, Iowa, have helped us. They've embraced our family with a generosity and an open-armed love that have convinced us they will continue to be there to support and help us in the raising of our children for years to come. Our wonderful community has been such an incredible part of our story that we can't imagine ever wanting to live anywhere else.

But a village isn't ever enough to raise a child.

That's why God created the concept of family. A mother and a father together. Two individuals becoming as one. A man and a woman who submit themselves to each other in love (Ephesians 5:21). Not in some fifty-fifty partnership, but each committing 100 percent—sometimes 110 percent—to each other, to their marriage, and to the otherwise impossible task of parenting.

God's idea of family extends far beyond a mother and father and siblings to include grandmas and grandpas and aunts and uncles and cousins who can multiply the love and the resources available for the raising of any child. Or seven. Or eight in our case.

We only *thought* we loved and appreciated our extended families before our septuplet adventure began. Words cannot express the debt of gratitude we owe for the immeasurable, uplifting, and sacrificial love our relatives have poured out on us before and since the birth of our babies. We have always counted on them, we count on them every day, and we know we can count on them as long as we live. For our families have not only given us life, they have provided a legacy of love that surrounds and upholds us in practical, everyday ways.

We know that in an increasingly mobile and rootless society like America's today, there are fewer and fewer extended families to help in the raising of children. That makes us all the more grateful for ours—and all the more convinced of the value of another often overlooked aspect of God's family master plan.

Many reporters who have covered our story don't quite know what to think of our commitment to church and our church's commitment to us. They view it as old-fashioned or quaint. The very idea of a *church family* strikes them as a cultural oddity, an intriguing, impractical, and mostly irrelevant remnant of the past that they're surprised to find still exists among the cornfields of Iowa.

Naturally we feel our church is something special—but only because it is ours. It would evidently surprise a lot of people to learn it isn't special at all. Yes, what our church family has done and continues to do for us is indeed extraordinary. Yet it is at the same time very ordinary.

Missionary Baptist Church of Carlisle, Iowa, is nothing more than what a church is supposed to be, what thousands of churches, not just here in the heartland, but around our country, still are—spiritual families bonded together not by genetics, by common upbringing, by long personal history, or even by shared cultural status. It's a far deeper, eternal bond—a bond of faith in a living, loving God and a mutual belief that one of the best ways to respond to the unspeakable love God offers us is to reflect and live out His brand of selfless, sacrificial, unconditional love to those around us.

Our church isn't perfect. No church is. Because it's made up of imperfect people like us.

But our experience, before the birth of our septuplets and certainly since, has convinced us that the biblical, Christian concept of a *church* is far from outdated. Indeed, the relationship we have with our church family has not only intrigued many people who've followed our story, it's been the object of envy for many.

This has helped convince us that, in a society as mobile as ours, so populated with single-parent households and so devoid of extended family contacts, the "old-fashioned notion" of belonging to a local body of believers may be more valuable today than at any point in history.

Raising a child today is certainly harder than it's ever been. Whether they have one child or a dozen, parents need all kinds of encouragement and practical help. Church families can and should provide such assistance. Thousands of them, like ours, do.

There is something more important and even more helpful than merely belonging to a local church family. It's knowing we're a part of the family of God and having a personal relationship with Him. It's knowing He has made us His heirs and will provide us an even more wonderful home for eternity—not because of anything we've done or could ever do, but simply because we have believed in His Son, Jesus Christ, as our Lord and Savior.

That automatically makes us part of God's family, provides us a very real and meaningful kinship with countless spiritual brothers and sisters here in Carlisle and around the world, and means He will be our heavenly Father forever.

That's not only the most crucial lesson we've learned in our lives; it's also the most important thing we want to teach our eight children. And it's the biggest reason we've written this book.

For our goal in putting our story into words on these pages is ultimately the same goal we have for our family. It's the same goal we set for ourselves and sang about at the very beginning of our lives together:

That . . . the whole world will know that we are a household of faith.